Gloria Hunniford was born in Northern Ireland and was the first woman to have her own daily radio show on BBC Radio 2, which she presented for thirteen years until 1993. She has appeared on and presented numerous shows including *Gloria Live, Wogan, Sunday Sunday, Heaven and Earth* and *Open House with Gloria* which gave Channel Five its highest ever ratings. She has won several prestigious awards, including TV Personality of the Year and a Lifetime Achievement Award. Gloria currently presents *Cash in the Attic* and *Rip-Off Britain*. She lives with her second husband, Stephen, in Sevenoaks, Kent, and together they have nine grandchildren.

GLORIOUS GRANDPARENTING

Grandparenting is not what it used to be, but as the grandmother to ten wonderful grandchildren, Gloria Hunniford knows about keeping up with them. In *Glorious Grandparenting* she shares her ideas on what to do when the grandchildren come to stay, and how to keep pace with them as they grow older. For many grandparents these days, life isn't always easy. In this book Gloria speaks to those who feel 'taken for granted' as a childminder, have conflicting views on childcare or, sadly, have become separated from their grandchildren. She looks at the controversial lack of legal rights for grandparents and offers advice and guidance on handling these emotive issues.

GLORIA HUNNIFORD

◆

GLORIOUS GRANDPARENTING

Complete and Unabridged

CHARNWOOD
Leicester

First published in Great Britain in 2010 by
Vermilion
an imprint of
Ebury Publishing, London

First Charnwood Edition
published 2011
by arrangement with
Ebury Publishing
A Random House Group company, London

The moral right of the author has been asserted

The names and some identifying details of the grandparents who share their experiences have been
changed in order to protect their privacy.

British Library CIP Data

Hunniford, Gloria, *1940 –*
Glorious grandparenting.
1. Grandparent and child.
2. Large type books.
I. Title
646.7′8–dc22

ISBN 978–1–4448–0832–2

Published by
F. A. Thorpe (Publishing)
Anstey, Leicestershire
Set by Words & Graphics Ltd.
Anstey, Leicestershire
Printed and bound in Great Britain by
T. J. International Ltd., Padstow, Cornwall

This book is printed on acid-free paper

CONTENTS

Introduction

I have just spent one of the most glorious and fulfilling days as a grandparent. Charlie, my eldest grandson, was celebrating his 16th birthday and the barbecue party held in his honour epitomised everything I believe in about the importance of the interchange between the family generations. On an occasion like this, with three generations together, laughing, enjoying one another, reminiscing and celebrating, there is a sense of completing the circle that is very special.

There is so much to be gained, as the older generation appreciates youth and all the energy and enthusiasm they bring to our lives. And for the grandchildren — apart from the love — there are the stories, family history and funny tales that a grandparent can pass on providing invaluable insights — not to mention fodder for endless teasing! Grandchildren adore hearing about just how naughty Mum or Dad was when growing up, or what they were like when they went to university or started their first job.

As I looked about on this sunny, landmark day at all of us sitting around a noisy long table, I realised that all sides of the family and extended family were represented. Charlie had his granny and granddad on his father's side and me and Stevie on his mum's side. There were uncles and aunts, great uncles and great aunts, cousins, his brother Gabriel, his half-sisters Tilly and newly born Flora, his stepmum Sally and her mother. There were also godparents, his mates and, all-important, his first serious girlfriend. There we all were, observing Charlie with total love and pride, while Charlie and his mates were probably observing us with mild embarrassment and tolerance.

After the meal it was time for the needle badminton tournament. I heard Charlie say, 'Here we go, the sixteen year olds up against the sixty year olds. Let's hope there are no heart attacks and that Stevie's new replacement knee doesn't cave in!' The smirk was on the other side of their faces when the sixty pluses won!

The one pivotal person who wasn't there was Charlie's mum, my gorgeous daughter Caron. Tragically Caron lost her ferocious seven-year battle with breast cancer six years ago and on a landmark day like a sixteenth birthday you can imagine how poignant that loss becomes. I felt incredibly sad that Caron wasn't around to see her fine son reach his sixteenth birthday, and with this in mind it seemed the right day to pass on to Charlie the Cartier watch that his dad had bought for his mum some years earlier. At the time she thought it was very posh, and thankfully it wasn't too girly looking. With its slim, rectangular face it suited Charlie well, and I had it engraved with his initials and the date of his birthday.

One of my other gifts to Charlie was a double photo album, chronicling his life from birth to the present time. I dated the sections with days, years and places, from where he was born in London, to moving to Cornwall from Barnes, and subsequently to Australia for three years, and then, after Mum died, to Hampton Court via another year in Fowey, Cornwall.

Charlie absolutely relished all the pictures, and as I watched him and his friends laughing hysterically at all the antics in the photographs, and the few bare bottoms I'd thrown in for good measure, it made me realise yet again that I am a truly important part of filling in his family history and his early life. I am a link — the only one left alive who knew his mum from birth to death. I also think, as Charlie now embarks on a new phase of his life, that the need to know what has gone before will become even more vital for him.

In putting together my birthday gift I was re-endorsing, to myself, how important a family link a grandparent can be on all levels, the pleasure involved in the exchange between grandchildren and grandparents and the realisation that, amidst all the joy my grandchildren bring me, I in turn have something to contribute to their lives and their being.

And that leads me to my reasons for writing this book. Being a grandparent is one of the great joys and privileges in life. For me it has been a journey of discovery, one I've embarked on with excitement, curiosity and wonder. Along the way, I have learned a great deal, both in my own life as a grandparent and about the experiences of other grandparents I have met and spoken to. It is this journey that I would love

3

to share, now, with those who are about to become grandparents as well as those who already are.

I firmly believe that we grandparents are a vital part of our grandchildren's lives — not just for the childcare and love we can offer and the gifts we bring, but for the stories, the hugs, the experience and of course the family history that we contribute. This is something I want to share, to celebrate and to encourage.

But there is another, sadder aspect of being a grandparent, which is also a very important issue. I was recently invited to become an ambassador of the Grandparents' Association, in my roles as both a grandmother and a broadcaster, an invitation I was delighted to accept. One of the first occasions I attended was a reception at 10 Downing Street intended to highlight the reasons why the Association is lobbying Parliament for greater legal rights for grandparents. I was shocked to hear the stories of those grandparents who, for various reasons, have been denied access to their grandchildren and who have '*no legal rights*' to redress this. Quite simply, grandparents in Britain have no legal rights. I am fortunate in that I see and talk to my grandchildren all the time, but for those who don't it must be deeply disturbing and devastating. So I very much wanted to help, by highlighting their situation and adding my voice to those pressing for a change in the law to allow grandparents the right to see their grandchildren. For this reason I have included some of their stories.

All grandparents should be able to see their grandchildren, and all grandparents can, if they choose to, make a positive and worthwhile contribution to their grandchildren's lives. Hearing the heartbreaking accounts of those grandparents who can no longer see their grandchildren made me even more appreciative of the good fortune most of us have in seeing our grandchildren regularly and sharing their lives as they grow up.

Being a parent was wonderful, and I wouldn't change it for the world. But being a grandparent is very special in a whole new way, as I discovered the day my first grandchild was born. Being a grandparent means the world to me — I am never happier than when I have my children and grandchildren around me at a big family gathering, which is why Charlie's special birthday party was such a joy.

This book is my reflection on the past sixteen years, with the highs, the lows, the laughter and tears and, most of all, the incredible learning curve that comes with this most special of roles — being a grandparent.

Holly aged 7
I Love my Nanny and grandad

1

From the Second You Were Born . . .

When I first realised I was going to be a grandmother I felt an extraordinary mixture of emotions: utter delight that my daughter Caron was pregnant, because it was something she had wanted very much; curiosity about the brand new person who would be joining our family; a small twinge of anxiety — would mother and baby come through it all healthy and well? — and hope that this little person would have a good life. But above all else I felt a great big wave of absolute joy and excitement. This was the start of a whole new journey in life for all of us — a journey of discovery and learning, and togetherness.

Caron and her husband Russ Lindsay had been married for two and a half years when they announced to the family, on Christmas Eve 1993, that Caron was two months pregnant. We were spending Christmas that year with family and friends in the New Forest in Hampshire and were gathered together for a Christmas Eve drink around the fire when Caron and Russ, with grins a mile wide on their faces, delivered their news. We all leaped up to give them hugs and kisses and danced and jigged around the room, then toasted the parents-to-be and the baby to come. It was a wonderful and special

7

Christmas present and a very happy time.

It wasn't until a little later that I had a moment to think about what it would mean for me and to take in the news that I was going to become a grandmother. What, I wondered, would that feel like, my daughter having a baby? I was nothing like my own grandparents had been when I was born, or even my parents when Caron was born. My mother and grandmother stayed at home to raise children, cook and look after the house. They had time to bake and make clothes and fuss over us. And although they weren't old when they became grandparents, they somehow seemed much older, because in those days the generations were much more clearly defined. For me, I realised, grandparent-hood would be very different; a whole new experience, and one I couldn't wait to begin.

Caron had suffered a miscarriage early in her marriage, so I was concerned that all should run smoothly in this pregnancy. And thankfully it did. She loved being pregnant, buying pretty maternity clothes, proudly showing off her bump and getting to know other mums-to-be. At that time Caron, who was 31 and a former *Blue Peter* presenter, was entertainment correspondent on *London Tonight*, the showbiz desk of the London News Network, which was part of ITN. Although she was an experienced television presenter by then, the job involved producing and editing her own films, skills she had yet to develop. So, by her own admission, Caron bluffed her way into it and learned as she went along. She was brilliant at live TV and delivering pieces straight to camera, and she soon got to grips with the editing process. Caron had natural warmth that she was able to put across, while at the same time being professional and accurate. She loved her job, and carried on working right through her pregnancy.

Russ headed up a management company with his friend Peter Powell, a former Radio 1 DJ. They named the company using their middle names — James and Grant — and launched it in 1984. They represented, and still do, a whole range of top showbiz, news and television names.

Russ was as excited as Caron about the baby. He couldn't wait to be a dad, and he and Caron got busy preparing a nursery in their home in Barnes with the latest trends in brightly coloured baby décor, and stocking up on everything from Babygros to cuddly toys. It was a time of delicious anticipation and all of us had enormous fun planning and preparing.

Of course I wanted to meet the baby as early as possible. I knew that when the time came I'd be hovering on the end of the phone as soon as Caron went into labour and I planned to rush to the hospital soon after the birth, relishing him as my first grandchild and longing to hold and snuggle him and give Caron and Russ a congratulatory hug. But in the end I was even luckier, because Caron asked me to be there at the birth. The day she asked, we were having lunch together. We often met for an early lunch, before we both went to work. I would head off to do my BBC Radio 2 early afternoon show and Caron went in the other direction to work on

9

London Tonight on the South Bank. It was a few weeks before the baby was due, and Caron was talking about the kind of birth she hoped to have.

'Would you like to be with Russ and me at the birth?' she asked. 'I'd feel happier with you there.'

It took me all of a split second to blurt out, 'I can't think of anything I'd love more. I'd be honoured and blessed.'

And I was. Being invited to be part of something so special felt like an enormous privilege, and such a contrast to my day, when not even husbands were allowed to be at the birth.

When the day came Russ rang me and told me it was all systems go and to meet them at the hospital, Queen Charlotte's in Chelsea. I dropped everything and raced over there, but I needn't have rushed: it was a long labour which went on right through the day. It was late July and very warm, so we spent most of the time getting her bottles of water and cooling cloths. While we waited for things to progress, Caron asked me what it had been like for me when she was a baby. I told her how her dad and I had come over to England from our home in Northern Ireland for a short break when I was almost eight months pregnant; it was to be my last jaunt before Caron was born. We went to see *Oliver!* and during the performance I went into labour and had to be rushed to hospital. Several weeks premature — she was in a hurry — Caron was tiny, but perfect. I had to wait a few weeks before flying home with her; I didn't feel safe, back then, flying with such a new baby, but my husband Don had had to return home to work, so instead of having him and my parents and friends around me, it was just Caron and me for those weeks, staying at a pal's house. That was tough and a bit lonely, but I adored my baby, and felt an incredibly close bond with her from the start.

Caron did want as natural a birth as possible, despite joking beforehand that her idea of natural birth was doing it without make-up! However, it was a long haul and as labour wore on she had an epidural and eventually it was decided that forceps would be needed to bring the baby into the world. At that point I decided to slip outside the room and give Caron and Russ a little privacy.

As I stood in the corridor I heard a woman screaming and hoped that Caron wasn't finding it as tough as the other woman obviously was. It was such a weird and at times panicky feeling, my little girl giving birth. I felt a huge wave of protectiveness. A few minutes later I was called back in, just in time to see the midwife cut the cord and place Caron's brand new son on her chest. Caron, exhausted from many hours in labour, looked down at him, smiled her beautiful wide smile, and said, 'Hello baby.' I'll never forget that moment; we were all in tears.

Minutes later I was able to say my own hello, as the baby was handed to me for my first cuddle. I looked down into his wide open, deep blue eyes and felt an overwhelming rush of joy and love.

Caron and Russ called him Charles — Charlie for short. The name featured strongly in both sides of the family; Russ's grandfather, my brother and my dad. When she was a little girl Caron adored her grandfather, and he absolutely worshipped her. So it was lovely to see the link being reinforced through her son.

I had never seen a baby born before. It sounds a bit daft to say that, when you've given birth to three, but when you're the mum you don't actually see a lot of what's going on at the other end. Watching from the sidelines was utterly magical — as I've said time and time again, nothing prepares you for being a grandparent.

Caron stayed in hospital for the next couple of days, getting used to breastfeeding, changing, bathing and caring for Charlie, before she and Russ brought him home to Barnes.

I visited every day, staying for as long as I could before dragging myself off to work, or coming in the evening after I finished my programme. Like the rest of the family, I was besotted with Charlie and couldn't wait to see him each day.

I was the world's proudest grandmother — now where have I heard that before? Within days I was wheeling him round Barnes in his pram, enjoying my new status, as friends and passers-by stopped to peer into the pram and coo at Charlie.

Caron was a natural mother; she took to it instantly and loved it. I had, I hope, always given her a positive attitude when it came to being a parent. Having children is the best thing I've ever done in my life, more important and fulfilling than everything else put together. I always told Caron that, so I think she was expecting a good experience, and that's certainly what it turned out to be.

For the next few weeks Caron and Russ's home was a bit like Piccadilly Circus, as friends and family all came to meet the new arrival. My sons, Paul and Michael — Caron's younger brothers — newly elevated to uncledom, came to meet their nephew. Russ's parents and brothers were there too, all of them new to the experience as well. And all Caron and Russ's work colleagues and friends arrived with baby gifts and goodies for the new parents.

Caron, wrapped up in the cycle of feeds and nappies and sleep deprivation, was tired but glowing. Russ was a fantastic hands-on dad from the start, so he and the rest of us would take over the changing, rocking, burping and lulling to sleep duties as often as we could, to give Caron a break.

Caron bounced back to her normal weight, and less than three months after Charlie's birth she went back to work, taking over from Fern Britton as presenter of *After 5*. This suited her perfectly. She enjoyed the programme, which involved both presenting and interviewing celebrities, and it meant that she could spend the mornings with Charlie and then be home from work in time to put him to bed.

For the next year and a half I continued to pop in to Caron and Russ's home most days, for a cup of tea, a quick cuddle with Charlie and endless chats with Caron. They also came to stay with me in Kent, certainly every other weekend. That way Caron and Russ could have a much-needed lie-in while I got up with Charlie. I've always been an early riser and I loved pottering around, enjoying him in the peace and quiet of the morning. We'd sit at the kitchen table with our colouring books and crayons, Charlie with his little spotted mug and me with a huge cup of tea.

At that time I had only recently got together with Stephen, my new partner. We had known one another for quite some time, and eventually the relationship grew into more than a friendship. After a few years as a lone parent, it was gorgeous to have someone to share the highs and lows of life with.

We had just moved in together when we had Charlie to stay for the first time. He was just a few weeks old, and we said we'd look after him so that Caron and Russ could get away for a couple of days. At one stage I brought Charlie into bed with us and Stephen and I looked at one another and said 'Instant baby!' then burst out laughing.

It was an immensely happy time, and that happiness increased when my son Paul and his partner Sandy told us before Charlie was a year old that they too were expecting their first child. Once again it was celebrations and toasts all round. By this time I knew just how good it felt to be a grandmother, and I couldn't wait to do it all over again.

Of course I had no expectation of being at the

birth; I just hoped to go and see the new baby as soon as Paul and Sandy were ready. But circumstances dictated otherwise!

The baby was due a couple of weeks after Christmas, and that year I had Caron and Paul and their families, as well as my youngest son Michael, staying for the holiday. With eight of us in the house, plus assorted guests arriving each day, it was a busy but lovely time, topped off by the sight of Charlie in a little red shirt which proclaimed 'my first Christmas' across the front. I am never happier than when I have my family around me, so I bustled around, shoving endless amounts of food into the oven and enjoying every minute of noisy togetherness.

On Christmas night, after a huge meal, lots of games and laughter and too many presents, we all fell into bed, exhausted. What felt like moments later, Paul was tapping me on the arm.

'Mum,' he said, 'Sandy's gone into labour.'

I dragged myself back from sleep and within minutes Stephen, Russ and Caron had been roused — though somehow we forgot to wake Michael, who slept through everything. What followed was a fantastic team effort; Russ scraped ice off the car and warmed the engine while Caron timed the contractions and I threw on my clothes and grabbed my car keys. I was in panto in Bromley at the time, with Christopher Biggins, and I had a show to do on Boxing Day, so I drove to the hospital separately in case I had to dash off.

They set off with Stephen driving, Sandy beside him, Paul, who was feeling really unwell

15

with flu, lying on the back seat and me tailing close behind.

Sandy kept saying to Stephen, 'I never thought I'd be racing around the M25 in labour, with you holding my hand'! Of course she had hoped to have her own mum there, but she was in Switzerland on holiday and couldn't get back in time, so when Sandy asked me to stay with her, of course I was only too thrilled to do so and once again felt privileged to be there.

Ironically Paul spent most of Sandy's labour lying on the floor, feeling like death warmed up and being tended to by the nurses, but when we were told that she would need a caesarean he rallied, got into a gown and mask, held her hand throughout and witnessed his first child being born. Needless to say, I never got as far as my performance as the fairy godmother in *Cinderella*, but somehow I felt the magic wand had been waved anyway as I saw my grandson Jake being born and, cuddling him a few minutes later, I felt the sheer happiness and thrill of being a grandparent for the second time. Eighteen months after Charlie's birth, almost to the day, I had another grandson, and he was healthy and absolutely beautiful: blond hair and vivid blue eyes.

In the following weeks Paul and Sandy often brought Jake to visit. They even brought him to see me in the panto; I've got a picture of me in my flowing, multicoloured fairy godmother dress and over-the-top headdress, cuddling this little bundle (I often wondered, did I put him off panto for life?). Inevitably I didn't see quite as

My Grandad is really
funny becouse his glasses
always fall off. His nose
is like a cherry on a cake,
And i love him!
By Joshua aged 8

much of him as I did of Charlie, because Caron and I seemed to get together more, while Sandy had her mother and family for support. But that only made it even more special when I did see them, and it was with enormous joy that I watched both Charlie and Jake grow into gorgeous toddlers. It brought back the great pride that I felt when I took my children to visit my parents' house. I wanted to show them off and I wanted them to know their grandparents and experience the feeling of a family circle. I always sensed that Caron and Paul felt that way too.

It wasn't long until Caron and Russ had another surprise. When Jake was only a few months old, and Charlie not yet two, they announced that they were expecting a second baby. They were keen to provide a sibling for Charlie and were delighted that his brother or sister would be only two and a half years younger.

This time pregnancy was a little tougher for Caron, simply because she now had not only a busy job, but a small son to look after. She was blessed, and she knew it; she had lots of help and a dream job as well as a loving family. But there were inevitably times when she got very tired.

The baby was due in January 1997. Christmas passed and we all had a wonderful time together. Caron's only disappointment was that her father, Don, didn't make it over from Northern Ireland to spend the holiday with us. Don and I had separated twelve years earlier and divorced a few years later, but we remained good friends and

Caron was still very close to her father. They enjoyed a chat every Saturday morning. They would both listen to *Loose Ends* on Radio 4 and then they'd have their telephone call, discussing the topics they'd just listened to and the week they'd had. Caron was looking forward to a holiday in Florida a few months later, with her dad joining her, Russ, Charlie and the new baby for a sunshine break.

A week or so before the baby was due, Caron's girlfriends threw her a baby shower. By this time she had stopped work and was preparing for the birth, once again hoping things would be as straightforward as possible.

Then the bombshell was dropped. Caron received a call to say her father had died suddenly of a heart attack. He had died peacefully, at home, sitting at the kitchen table, drinking a glass of wine and reading the paper, but Caron was completely devastated, as were Paul and Michael. Paul's company travelled the world to set up sound systems for concerts and other major events and he was in Thailand when he got the news, so he had to endure a seemingly endless trip home. Michael was in London, as was Caron, and I got the news as I came off-set in Belfast, after presenting a live celebrity TV chat show.

Normally when a programme finishes there is a little bit of backslapping and 'that was marvellous, darling' that goes on, but despite the fact that I felt it had gone well, there was nothing. In fact it seemed as though people were avoiding my eyes. I was beginning to wonder

19

whether the programme had been awful, when I was siphoned off into a small dressing room and given the news. It was such a shock for all of us and I worried for all three of my children, but I knew that for Caron, in her hugely pregnant state, it was going to affect her on so many different levels.

Caron insisted on flying back to her old home in Hillsborough, near Belfast, where she had spent so many happy years with her dad and family. She shouldn't have been flying at her stage of pregnancy, but she hid her bump under a huge coat and boarded the plane with Russ. I was waiting for them in Belfast, and Caron fell into my arms, sobbing. It was a hugely emotional and draining time for all, and for Caron the timing couldn't have been worse.

She flew back to England a day later, and asked the doctors to induce her baby, so that she could then fly back to Belfast to attend her father's funeral. Looking back it seems like madness to keep rushing back and forth, but Caron wanted the familiarity of the hospital where she had Charlie and knew the staff, and she also wanted to say goodbye to her dad. In hindsight we should have just delayed the funeral, but at the time in our numb state none of us thought of doing that. So it was that her second baby was born on 28 January, just four days after her father had died.

Once again Caron asked me to be there; she needed me. This time I was grateful that she had because I wanted to give her all the support possible. It was another long and tiring labour and Caron was incredibly brave. When her second son, Gabriel arrived, we were all moved to tears of relief and joy. He was a beautiful baby, and Caron and Russ chose Don as his middle name, after her dad. As I held him and looked into his small, seemingly wise face all I could think was that he knew nothing of all the events surrounding his birth, and that I wanted to protect him from the grief and sadness that was, inevitably, part of that time.

There is no doubt that when you are present at the birth of a child there is an extra layer to the bond between you. In the years to come I was so glad and grateful for this bond with my grandsons. I used to say to them, 'I have loved you from the second you were born.' In fact I said it so much that when I began, 'I have loved you . . . ' they would chant back, 'I know Nana, from the second I was born.'

Caron and Russ were delighted to have another son, but this time she didn't have the luxury of a peaceful time at home, just getting to know her baby and recovering from the birth. When Gabriel was six days old we all flew back to Northern Ireland for Don's funeral. It was a deeply poignant moment, watching Caron attend the funeral with her new baby in her arms, swaddled in a blanket. She was heartbroken that she couldn't show Don his grandson.

What followed was a difficult time in which Caron never got the full joy of her baby's birth, or the full grief of losing her dad. Much of the time she didn't know whether to laugh or cry.

She should have been enjoying her new baby,

but while her love for him was in no doubt, she struggled to cope, finding it difficult to sleep and to concentrate on anything and becoming tearful and moody. The overwhelming emotions of birth and death intermingling left her with postnatal depression that lasted for many months. As a mother and grandmother I was deeply concerned both for her and Russ and for her two boys. I visited as often as I could, doing my best to help and to encourage her back to health. I know that many new mothers find themselves coping with postnatal depression, and many grandparents feel deeply anxious, as I did, about the effects of this, and how best to help. It's a subject I will return to in a later chapter, as one of the often unexpected difficulties families with new babies can face.

★   ★   ★

The year after Don's death and Gabriel's birth was a difficult one, and in marked contrast to the previous two years, after Charlie's birth, when it had seemed as though everything was close to perfect. Now the whole family was grieving; Don had only been 61 and his death had been so shockingly sudden, with no warning at all. But while I felt grief myself, and I knew our sons were bereft, my deepest concern at that time was for Caron, because she seemed much more vulnerable. She had sailed through the time after Charlie's birth, but now she struggled with normal life. What was never in doubt, however, was how much she adored Gabriel. We all did.

We fussed over him and, as you might expect, often reflected on that old adage about birth and death. Once again I was pushing a pram around Barnes and buying little granny presents. Charlie loved having a baby brother, and it was a joy to spend time with the two of them.

Gabriel was christened in the summer, and by that time Caron seemed much better. She was beginning to get back to her old self, and we all felt very optimistic. Heartbreakingly, it was soon after that, in September, less than nine months after Gabriel was born, that Caron found a lump in her breast which at first we and the doctors thought was just a milk lump. To our complete devestation a biopsy showed it to be cancerous. It was horrendous and one of the worst days of my life. I felt as though I had been hit by a truck. And for Caron, just 34, young, bright and beautiful, it was a complete and utter shock. At that stage I didn't know any young girls who'd had breast cancer and didn't know what to expect — I was so scared. But doctors assured us that it had been caught early and there was every chance of a full recovery. We felt certain that they were right, and she would soon put the whole, awful episode in perspective.

For the next few months I made myself put my fears aside, support Caron, spoil my grandchildren and trust that all would be well. Then just over a year after Gabriel's birth, in February 1998, we had lovely, positive news: Paul and Sandy were to have another baby. It was raining grandchildren! This would be my fourth in as many years, and I felt truly blessed.

The prospect of another baby in the family was a hugely happy one; we all had something to look forward to and a reason to celebrate.

There was a second celebration that year as well. Stephen and I were very happy together, we knew we had both found the person we wanted to share our lives with, so when he asked me to marry him I was thrilled and had no hesitation in saying yes. We had planned our wedding for early September, and when Paul and Sandy told us their baby was due around the same time we hoped he or she might make it to the wedding along with our other grandchildren.

In marrying Stephen I became step-grandmother to four more children, and we wanted to have all four of them, plus my three grandsons, as pages and bridesmaid.

Stephen has two sons, Dominic and Matthew, and between them they had four children at that time — a fifth, little Lily, has since arrived. Elicia, the oldest, was six, Elliot was five and identical twins Jake and Billy were three. That gave us six boys aged five and under between us. Elicia, as the only girl and the eldest, got to dress up in a fairytale dress and lead the pages behind her.

I loved getting to know Stephen's grandchildren, and he embraced mine — and my children — with such warmth and generosity that I was deeply touched. Stephen has a big heart, and throughout the difficult years that were to follow, with Caron's illness, he was steadfast in his support and love for me, for her and for the whole family.

We married at St Peter's church close to Hever Castle in Kent, not far from our home in Sevenoaks. It was the church my children and I had adopted when we moved to England from Northern Ireland in 1982 and was where Caron and Russ had married seven years earlier. Hever Castle, with its famous Italian gardens, where we held Caron and Russ's reception and then mine and Stephen's, was a beautiful venue that we all loved. Stephen and I stayed there the night before, and at about nine that evening Paul arrived in the middle of our pre-wedding dinner to tell us the wonderful news that Sandy had just given birth to another boy, named Beau. It was the ultimate wedding gift; we were thrilled, and couldn't wait to see him.

In a good old-fashioned way, we slept in separate rooms, and at six in the morning I got up and padded into the corridor with a cup of tea, planning to wake Stephen and say, 'Let's go and see the new baby.' Outside my room I met Stephen, padding down the corridor towards my room, with a cup of tea in his hand and the same idea. We laughed, downed the tea and rushed off to the hospital to meet little Beau, who was gorgeous, contented and perfect in every way. A tired but happy Sandy wished us well for our wedding day. She was disappointed that she wouldn't see Jake going down the aisle in his pageboy outfit, but we promised to take lots of photos and to celebrate with her and Paul as soon as we got back from honeymoon.

That day I walked down the aisle with my seven grandchildren behind me, picturing the eighth in his mother's arms in hospital, and I felt truly happy and contented. Between us we had a wonderful big family, the kind every Irish mother, and grandmother, delights in. I felt very humble, extremely fortunate and thankful.

My Grandma

Grandma is brilliant,
Shes pretty with candy floss
hair and a big crocodile smile

Grandma →

Me

Grandad

My Grandad

My grandad is the
most wonderful grandad,
We visit when the sun
shines and have big
BBQs. It's funny when gran-
-dad holds onto my ear!

2

Becoming a Grandparent

When I knew I was going to be a grandmother several journalists asked me how I felt. I told them I was very, very excited, but that I didn't really want to be called Granny, thanks very much. I felt I was too young for the 'Granny' tag which, at that stage, seemed to conjure up pictures of grey-haired old ladies, rocking chairs, scratchy knitted jumpers and hearing aids. But the moment my first grandson, Charlie, was born, I was so besotted I couldn't have cared less what I was called. Suddenly a whole, wonderful stage of life was opening up before me, filled with wonders and possibilities.

In the end my grandchildren called me Nana, and every time I heard it I felt fresh pleasure. I still do, although one day recently I heard a deep voice saying 'Hello Glo,' and when I turned around it was Charlie. That's something else; it signifies that he's really growing up, and the subtle changes in our relationship that go with it. Grandparents come with many different names. I love the word grandmother — it reminds me of the famous quote by an unknown author, 'It's such a grand thing to be a mother of a mother — that's why the world calls her grandmother.' And of course the same is true for grandfather.

I know grandparents who are called the

traditional Granny and Granddad, or Grandma and Grandpa, or Nana, as I and many others are. But there are so many names that families use, and many just choose or invent their own. I know a Grammy, a Ganji and a Gangan. And for grandfathers I've come across Poppy, Gramps, Grampa, Granda and my father was Grando.

Then there are the names used in other cultures, many of them very beautiful and some of which are sometimes adopted into ours. For the Italians a grandmother is Nonna and the grandfather is Nonno, in Greece she's Yaya and he's Papou, in Spain she's Tita and he's Tito, in China she's Nai-nai and he's Yeh-yeh, in Iceland she's Amma and he's Afi, in India she's Nanni and he's Daada, in Russia it's Babushka and Dedushka and in Israel Bubbe and Zeydeh, while in Swahili she's Bibi and he's Babu and in Gaelic she's Mammo and he's Daddo.

There are many more, in many cultures around the world, and what all these wonderful names have in common is that they are easy for small children to pronounce and somehow resonant with love and familiarity. These names spell comfort and warmth and it's easy to imagine little children all over the world calling out to their grandparents and running into their arms.

Some grandparents will know exactly what they want to be called; others will simply find that a name emerges from their grandchild's attempts to say their name, or 'Grandma' and 'Grandpa'. But whatever you're called, this name signifies a new role in your life, and one that is of the utmost importance, value and joy.

Now, more than ever before, grandparents play an important part in family life. Why now more than ever? Because there are more of us, and we live longer, so we're far more likely to be part of our grandchildren's lives than in the past.

Today, in Britain, there are estimated to be 14 million grandparents. The youngest is an eye-watering 28, while the oldest is over 100. But most of us become grandparents in our late forties or early fifties, and by the age of 54 over half of us have a grandchild.

Because we live so much longer than in the past, most children today will know what it is to have grandparents, and many will have a grandparent in their lives for 25 years or even longer. That gives us the possibility of a long, warm and loving relationship quite different to any other in our lives.

They often say that having grandchildren is even better than having children, because you feel the same unconditional love, yet the discipline, routine and hard work are not ultimately yours. If you're lucky, you just get to spoil them, love them, play with them and then hand them back.

It was Erma Bombeck, the American newspaper columnist and humorist, who said, 'If I had known grandchildren were going to be so much fun, I'd have had them first.' And writer Gore Vidal echoed that, saying, 'Don't have children, only grandchildren,' while cartoonist Mell Lazarus said, 'The secret of life is to skip having children and go directly to grandchildren.'

I can't quite agree. I absolutely adore my grandchildren, but I loved being a mother too and, as I've said before, it was the best and most important role in my life; I wouldn't swap it for the world. Parenthood is hugely rewarding, and at the same time not a day went by when I didn't worry about one of my children for some reason or other. As a grandmother I love my grandchildren just as deeply as I loved my children. And of course I've worried too, but less than I did when all the responsibility was mine, 24 hours a day. Freed of some of the day-to-day practicalities, I have been able to revel in the sheer delight of being with them.

Many of the other grandparents I have met and spoken to agree with this. 'Nothing prepared me for what I felt when I held my grandchild in my arms for the first time,' said Irene, who became a grandmother at the age of 48. 'It was extraordinary; I just felt such a rush of love, and protectiveness. It didn't make me feel old at all; it made me feel there was suddenly an extra reason to stay young, fit and healthy.'

It isn't just our children's birth children who wrap themselves around our heartstrings. Dianne's grandchildren are adopted. 'My grandson was adopted at three months old, and two years later my daughter and her husband adopted a second child, a little girl who was a year old and had been in foster care. I had no idea how I would feel about being a grandparent to adopted babies, but I found it made not a jot of difference. I probably feel a little more protective than usual, because I know they both started life in difficult circumstances, but in all other respects I'm the same as every other grandmother I know — besotted! And I'm secretly delighted when people tell me they are more like me than their adoptive parents!'

Families come together in many different ways these days. I recently met a distinguished Jewish accountant who told me that his lawyer daughter and her female partner had very much wanted to have children together. A gay male friend offered to help, and using artificial insemination each of the two women had a baby by him — one a boy and the other a girl. They now have a very happy family, with two mums and two children and a father who adores both children and shares the childcare. He takes both children every other weekend and his mother, who thought she would never become a grandmother, is thrilled because she now has two grandchildren and sees them often. The grandfather who told me this story was also delighted that he has two more grandchildren to add to his fold. So what might have been seen as somewhat unconventional a few years back is now totally accepted within this loving and extended family.

Another grandmother I came across recently told me her single daughter had given birth to a gorgeous little boy after a very brief relationship. The daughter, a professional woman with a successful career and a good income, was happy to have her baby on her own and well able to provide for him. The baby's father was no longer on the scene, sadly, but the grandparents and two uncles were all very close to the little boy and very involved with his upbringing.

These two stories provide just two examples of the kaleidoscope that reflects relationships and family setups in today's world. All kinds of situations which might previously have been considered unusual are now totally normal. And when families are inclusive and loving, children thrive.

This is something that applies to cultures from around the world. Cecilia has six grandchildren. 'In the Afro-Caribbean community we treasure grandchildren, and I cried a bucket of tears and gave thanks each time one of my grandchildren was born,' she says. 'There is something very special about seeing your family carry on growing and extending.

'I live a few doors away from both my daughters and I see my grandchildren every day. My daughters work, so the children come to me after school and I feed them all, check their homework and bath them before they go home. I couldn't imagine it being any other way.'

Not all grandparents are as lucky as Cecilia, in having their grandchildren so close by. And geography does make a huge difference. Donna, who lives in Ireland, knows all about this, because she has grandchildren close by and far away.

'I have a daughter living across the road,' she says, 'and another living in England. So I have two grandchildren coming in and out of my house, I see them every day, and there are two more I only see two or three times a year. I do my very best to keep close to them, I send little cards and presents and phone them and I love having them over. But inevitably I am closer to the children who are here daily. I know about their friends, their hopes and dreams, how they're doing at school and what they are saving their pocket money for.'

Even those in exalted positions revel in the sheer delight of becoming grandparents. Former Prime Minister Margaret Thatcher famously announced, when her son Mark became a father, 'We are a grandmother.' It may have sounded a little over-regal, but the broad smile on her face gave away the pleasure she felt.

The Queen first became a grandmother at the age of 52 when her daughter, Princess Anne, gave birth to her son Peter Phillips in 1977; she now has eight grandchildren and, at the age of 84, is set to be a great-grandmother when Peter and his wife Autumn's first child is born in December 2010.

And what of grandfathers? Is it just as magical for them?

'It certainly is,' says Ted, who has been a grandfather for five years. 'I have one or two friends who didn't feel strongly about becoming grandfathers; they were men who'd always kept pretty distant from their own children, and they were expecting to be the same with their grandchildren. One of them told me, 'I'm not really the kiddie type.' I felt sorry for him because he didn't know what he was missing. Children, if you let them close, bring untold joy and fulfilment. My wife and I have our granddaughter over all the time and we love it;

she makes me laugh and she gives me an excuse to play games. I think I'm still a big kid at heart.'

Ted's friend isn't the only grumpy granddad (and I'm sure there are some grumpy grandmas too). Writer Martin Amis said that learning he was about to become a grandfather was 'like getting a telegram from the mortuary'. What a twist, to see it that way; we all know we're growing older anyway, but if you enjoy your grandchildren you have a lot less time in which to worry about it.

Spike Milligan, the great comedian, once said that having grandchildren was 'like a beautiful injection of sadness'. I think he meant that there was beauty in the very existence of this lovely child, but sadness in the sudden realisation that here was someone you would worry about for the rest of your life.

There can be sadness, too, in becoming a grandparent once your partner in life is no longer there to share it with you.

The birth of Joanna's granddaughter was a bittersweet time, because it came two years after Joanna's husband Peter died.

'Peter wanted grandchildren more consciously than I did,' Joanna says. 'When our son was still in his early twenties Peter used to say to him, 'When am I going to have a grandchild?' We were together for 37 years, and although he was 20 years older than me I thought he would live into his nineties, as his parents had, and I hoped we would enjoy grandchildren together. When he died I felt a terrible sense of loss. I retreated into my work, as a publisher, and kept busy.

Grampy gardens everyday day because he loves his home grow vegetables.

When we go for walks with the dog, he tells me funny stories.
by Joseph Coates age nine

'When our granddaughter Meg was born it was a time of such joy, but for me it was also tinged with sadness, because Peter wasn't there to share it.

'On all those special occasions, like birthdays, I'm so aware that Peter isn't here. He would have loved Meg, and I find myself looking for him in her; she's cuddly, and funny and feisty, as he was, and she loves to play little games and tease — Peter was a great tease and so often had a twinkle in his eye.

'I think of Meg as Peter's grandchild, even more than mine. If I feel sad because I've lost Peter, I think, 'Now I've got little Meg, she's his descendant,' and I feel better. And after two and a half years of being very self-sufficient, it's lovely to be needed again, and to have a new role to play.'

That new role can take on so many dimensions. And what many grandparents discover is that with the arrival of their grandchildren they have another chance to do things right in life. So many young parents are busy building a life, a career, a home that they can sometimes be short on time for their children. I know quite a number of people who feel sad, looking back, that they didn't chat to their children more, play with them, take meandering walks, make daisy chains and listen to their stories of life at school, their worries and their hopes and dreams.

With grandchildren there is a chance to do some of those things, not simply because there may be more time — many grandparents are still working and still pretty busy — but because you don't have to do the day-to-day care, and so the time you do have with them can be spent in other ways. You can make time to play, to listen, to wander and to really know and understand this little person in a way you may not have with your own children.

There's another wonderful knock-on effect of becoming a grandparent. Many report that their relationship with their own children improves greatly with the birth of a grandchild. This is not just because they may be needed, to help out. It's because when a young adult becomes a parent for the first time they suddenly realise what it must have been like for their own parents — it suddenly clicks into place.

I remember this so well myself. I had my first baby, Caron, at the age of 22, my second, Paul, at 24 and my youngest, Michael, at 31. When Caron was born I remember feeling that I understood my mum and dad more deeply than I ever had before. I realised what it was to love a child and the responsibility that came with new life. All those times I thought my mother was being unreasonable, she was simply motivated by the love and protectiveness I was now feeling.

I wanted to go off to Canada and visit my intriguing great-uncle, and when I was 17 I did. My mother wasn't happy, but it wasn't, as I felt then, because she was unfair, or trying to hold me back, it was because she worried about me being thousands of miles away and didn't want anything to happen to me. This realisation made me softer and more understanding towards my mother. I saw through her eyes, and that was a gift. It made me more patient and tolerant.

I had always been close to my mum; the birth of my own children simply gave me another, deeper layer to my understanding of who she was. But for parents and children whose relationship has been thorny and difficult, a grandchild can bring healing and understanding.

Maura and her daughter Niki had a difficult relationship ever since Niki was a teenager. 'She was such a lovely little girl,' Maura says, 'but at 15 she ran away from home, lived in a squat, left school and refused to speak to me and her dad. We were devastated and felt she was ruining her life. We tried to reach her, but she felt we were the enemy and for three years we barely saw her. During that time we had to trust that she would come back to us, but it was hard. Then a few years ago she got back in touch and told us she had a job and a flat and was trying to make up the education she'd missed. Things were still a bit prickly between us, until last year she had a son. She called me as she was in labour, and I rushed to the hospital, where we hugged and cried and our relationship began to truly heal over this adorable little boy. I think no matter what the circumstances, every woman wants her mother at the birth.

'Since then we've grown much closer. I help Niki and her partner out by having my grandson as often as I can, and Niki and I are much closer. A couple of months ago she told me that she understood why I was so angry and frightened when she ran away. That meant a lot.'

As Maura, and many others, have found, the arrival of a grandchild can bring healing to a fractured family.

If adult children begin to understand their parents better, there's also a big emotional adjustment for the grandparent that comes with seeing your child become a parent. I remember feeling that my children were really grown up once they settled into long-term relationships, with homes of their own. But it wasn't until the first grandchild arrived that I really knew they were adult. Somehow when your child has a child of their own, it marks a significant shift in the relationships all along the chain. You look on in wonder as your child produces a child and takes on all the responsibility that goes with that momentous event, and at that point you metaphorically have to take a step back and realise they have their own lives to live, they can manage and that your role has to change in response to that.

Just as Caron, when she was in labour, wanted to know about my experience of becoming a mum, I looked at her after Charlie's birth and thought, 'You're a different person now, a mother yourself.' I saw her through new eyes; I felt a deep surge of respect for her after watching her go through labour; I saw that she was a woman and not my little girl any longer. It was the same with my son Paul: when his first son was born I realised that he was a man, a father, with all that entails, and while I loved him just as deeply I felt a deeper level of understanding for him.

Not that I have ever stopped worrying and feeling protective towards my children, or wanting to move heaven and earth for them if things get tough. I didn't used to think I had a bigger well of protectiveness in me, but once my grandchildren arrived I found the protectiveness I felt towards my children was tripled towards my grandchildren. I understood more about the vulnerability of life and all that goes with it.

I mentioned at the beginning of this chapter that my idea of a granny at one point before I became one was just a tad old-fashioned and stereotypical. How many grannies today are actually old, in rocking chairs, knitting scratchy jumpers — or even grey-haired? And how many grandpas are grumpy old men, sitting in a favourite armchair with their pipe and slippers? Not a lot.

So who are grandparents today? Well, it's definitely time to shake off the preconceptions and outdated images. The vast majority of grandparents now are leading extremely full and active lives, after all the government say we don't have to retire at the age of 65. We work, exercise, travel, go on dates, go surfing, climb mountains, dance, write books, run businesses and generally pack in a huge amount of living.

Age has changed, we all know that. Forty used to be quite old, now it's not even middle-aged. Fifty is cool, and sixty, far from being the pensionable age, is just a blip in our otherwise full and rewarding lives. We don't grow old waiting to die, as so many did in the past, we grow old while still living life to the full and savouring every moment. We are far less set in our ways than our own grandparents. We may know what we like in life — a distinct advantage — but we are also excited about experimenting, whether that's with exotic food, new languages, new places to live or a new look.

I came across a great little poem that sums up the way grandparents have changed.

Grandma's Off Her Rocker!
(By unknown author)
In the dim and distant past,
When life's tempo wasn't fast,
Grandma used to rock and knit,
Crochet, tat and babysit.
When we were in a jam,
We could always count on gram.
In the age of gracious living,
Grandma's life was one of giving.
But today . . .
Now grandma's at the gym,
Exercising to keep slim,
She's off touring with the bunch,
Or taking all her friends to lunch.
Driving north to fish or hike,
Taking time to ride her bike.
Nothing seems to block or stop her,
Now that grandma's off her rocker.

Thanks to better nutrition and medical care, plus a far greater knowledge and understanding of what is good for us, most of us can live longer than our grandparents dreamed was possible. And we can really live — we don't have to sit in an armchair knitting, wear floral crimplene dresses or have that blue rinse. Now we can take up salsa dancing, cook a paella, have a sexy bob and buy a chic little dress. The choices and options open to us are vast and life-enhancing. Most of us are reasonably financially stable, and you don't have to be well off to have a good and interesting life. There are so many things to be part of, contribute to and enjoy, so many books to read, exhibitions to see, exciting things to learn on the internet, friends to laugh with and enjoy.

Certainly for me being a grandparent has marked a wonderfully positive stage of my life. I feel more comfortable in my skin and more fulfilled than I have ever been before. I'm less anxious, less easily embarrassed, more relaxed and a better cook! I've loved watching my family grow, like the branches of a tree spreading out. It's a good feeling, knowing that the torch will be carried on, long after I'm gone.

These days every other person is a grandparent, and proud of it. Look at Hollywood — Jim Carrey became a grandfather this year at the age of 48, Donny Osmond is a grandfather (yes, really) and so is Lionel Richie. As for Steve Tyler of the band Aerosmith, father of the gorgeous Liv, he has to be one of the sexiest grandfathers ever. And he won a whole new generation of fans the day he went down on one knee and gently serenaded his three-year-old grandson during one of his concerts.

Harrison Ford and Goldie Hawn were recently voted Hollywood's hottest grandparents, while in the grandma camp there is also Priscilla Presley, who joined the club at 44, Tina Turner, Sally Field and Whoopi Goldberg, who became a grandma at the astonishing age of 34, after having a daughter at 18 who then had a child at 16. Whoopi is 54 now and must be well on the way to becoming a great-grandma.

Then don't forget, closer to home, granddads Mick Jagger (plus the rest of the Stones), Paul McCartney (who now has six grandchildren), Pierce Brosnan (he became a grandfather at 44, six years after being voted the 'Sexiest Man Alive') and Sean Connery, plus glamorous grandmas Joanna Lumley, Felicity Kendal, Marianne Faithfull and Charlotte Rampling. It's on record that they all love being grandparents, and it certainly hasn't stopped them being rock stars or actors and having massive fan followings.

A few months ago Stephen and I went to see Paul McCartney performing in London's Hyde Park. Sitting in front of us was Paul's daughter, Stella — who, incidentally, was named after both her grandmothers — with her son, Beckett, who was then about 18 months old. I had to smile to myself, because all little Beckett wanted was to get up on stage with his granddad. He jumped and wriggled around and Stella told us he loved his grandfather's music. How cool is that for Paul?

It's funny, given that we all know 'older' isn't the same as it used to be, that a fair few of us still think of a grandparent as 'old' and think that when we become one it means we are certainly

45

getting older. I did this, I know, but since then I have learned to look at things differently and I have come to think of becoming a grandparent as entering a third age in life. My first age was pre-children, my second was being a young adult, with marriage, a busy career and children, and my third is being a grandmother, with marriage, a busy career and grandchildren. I hope I'm a little wiser, calmer and more understanding than I was when I was younger, but apart from that not a lot has changed. Except that now I don't have to be a day-to-day, hands-on parent, I can be a loving, interested, supportive (I hope) and occasionally wickedly indulgent grandmother. And it's the most fun I've ever had.

There's a lovely quote from American novelist and poet Christopher Morley: 'It is as grandmothers that our mothers come into the fullness of their grace.' I think that says so much about life, and about growing older, if you do it with acceptance, a spring in your step and genuine joy at the inevitable changes that come about. If you can laugh at your wrinkles while treasuring your grandchildren, then I think you've got the balance right.

I firmly believe that being a grandparent brings out the best in us. It makes us less selfish, more generous, more youthful and wiser. Because we are one step back from being parents, we can see so much more clearly. We know that rows will be resolved, lost toys eventually found and that most things come right in the end.

Being grandparents give us a chance for a fresh, energising take on life, and an opportunity to be loved by a small person to whom you hope you will always be special. What could be grander than that?

My Granny!

My Crinkily Wrinkily granny always loves to cook, but sometimes

OUch!

she maniges to burn herself.

OUch!

Madeline, 9years

3

A Wonderful Model

I grew up with the most wonderful grandparents and, along with my parents, they provided me with a model of how to be a really loving, hands-on grandparent. Not that they were aware, at the time, of giving me a model. They were simply being their usual, loving selves.

A grandparent can play a pivotal role in their grandchildren's lives, providing so much that is precious and important in those early years. Yet setting out on grandparenthood for the first time can seem quite daunting. So if you're lucky enough to have known your grandparents, and had a good relationship with them, it's a great advantage.

Mine was a very traditional Irish upbringing. My father, Charlie, was in charge of the advertising department of a newspaper, and my mother, May, stayed at home to look after me and my sister Lena, who was seven years older than me, and my brother Charles, who was seven years younger. My siblings and I were convinced our parents only 'did it' every seven years!

I was loved and I always knew it. How fortunate was that! My parents were not well off, money was tight, but they were good, honest people who gave me and my brother and sister lots of affection, hugs and kisses. My mother would bake endlessly and Dad grew all our own vegetables. He was very practical and could make or mend anything, from dolls' furniture to bicycles. He was also very bright, despite having left school at 13, and wrote and painted beautifully.

Dad was also a semi-professional magician in his spare time, and in those pre-TV days he was a big name on the homespun Irish entertainment circuit, appearing regularly in church halls and school venues — all good, innocent fun. He was magical on stage and magical to watch and we were very proud of him. From the age of eight I used to perform too, as a singer. Dad and I would travel to what were called Ham Suppers and Daffodil Teas, where there would be tables bedecked with flowers and laden with local produce and home-made food, and after everyone had eaten we would provide the entertainment, under the banner of the Mid-Ulster Variety Group.

At home Dad was a strict disciplinarian. You weren't allowed to swear in our house and if you did you were threatened with being put out of the house. Once I broke the rule when I had just washed my hair and had it in a towel. It was winter and very cold, but my father showed me the door. My mother was worried sick, but my father said, 'She knew the rules,' and he stuck by his principles. But of course I simply went to a neighbour's and sat in their house until I was allowed back in!

My grandparents on both sides were very much a part of the family setup. On my mother's

50

side I had only my grandmother, as my mother's father had died young. My grandmother, who was always known as Granny McCann, was a wonderful, big, strong Trojan of a woman. She came from a fairly well-off family that had a sizeable farm in the country. My grandparents only had two children, my mother and her brother, Roy, and they were used to fine things and were well looked after.

Granny McCann came from the country to visit us in Portadown every Wednesday and Saturday, without fail, and she would sit in the corner of our sitting room, watching through the window as people went by. She lived a fairly isolated existence on the farm; it was down at the end of a country lane, so nobody ever passed by except the locals, and she was fascinated by the bustle of the town.

My lasting memory is of her saying to my mother, 'May, who's that going by?' She thought we knew everyone, but of course we had no idea who it was most of the time. We lived near to the football ground and on a Saturday she loved watching all the football fans going to the match.

Granny McCann was a great source of treats to us children. When I was little I loved having brand new white ankle socks to go with my Clarks sandals. She would say, 'Would you like some nice new socks?' and then produce them — lacy socks that clung to the ankle where the elastic was still tight. I thought they were wonderful.

The farm where Granny McCann lived with her son was about five miles outside town and we often used to cycle over there to visit her. My father didn't drive, and in any case we couldn't have afforded a car, so we went everywhere on bikes. In those days we didn't have helmets or special seats; I just sat on a cushion strapped to the back of my father's bike, until I was big enough to ride a bike of my own.

My mother liked to visit her mother often, and in the summers before my brother came along my sister would stay at the farm all through the holidays. I would insist I wanted to stay too, but when my parents got up to go home on their bikes I started to cry, changed my mind and said I wanted to go home with them.

When I was older I did stay, and it was such a treat. Granny McCann had a donkey which we used to ride bareback. So she had to have a good supply of sticky plasters. The farm grew lots of fruit, there were great orchards of Bramley apples; I never look at one, even now, without thinking of my childhood. In the spring there would be acres of apple-blossom and the scent was heavenly. My uncle would come into the huge flagstoned kitchen with boxes of damsons, apples and pears, while my mother preserved the pears in big jars and made the damsons into jam.

There were always a couple of big, black pots dangling from the crook in my grandmother's big, open farmhouse kitchen. One would be full of swill for the pigs, and the other full of soup or stew for us.

I remember the haymaking in the summer, the huge piles of hay and getting a ride on the hay wagon. One of my most lasting memories is of my grandmother, this Trojan woman, marching through the fields to where the men were working, gathering the hay. She would be carrying a big wicker hamper and when she set it down and opened it up there would be soda farls and potato farls (flat round loaves cut into quarters) just off the griddle, with butter oozing through them, and pots of home-made jam. It would all be washed down with great big mugs of tea. It was absolute heaven.

When I look back on those days, it's as though the sun was always shining. And then at the end of the day we'd climb into Granny's big brass bed with its feather pillows and eiderdown and snuggle down, warm and cosy, while the lamps made dancing shadows on the wall. There was no electricity then so we managed with open fires and paraffin lamps.

If we were at the farm on Sundays we went to church in a beautiful shiny cart, pulled by a pony. Granny McCann had been brought up a Quaker and she still went to church every Sunday. I remember climbing up into the cart and sitting up very straight, feeling proud, as we trotted along.

Granny had a brother, Jim, who had run off to Canada when he was 19. No-one heard from him again, until one day, when I was eight or nine, he reappeared. I came up the path to the house to see this majestic-looking man, as tall as my grandmother, with a fabulous shock of white hair. He had made his fortune in electronics and had come back to look for his family, whom he hadn't seen for 40 years.

He regaled us with tales of Canada, which I thought sounded like the land of milk and honey — especially as, being just after the war, we still had rationing. He made it sound wonderful, and when he invited me to visit I was desperate to go there. But my mother, quite understandably, said no. I was furious and determined to go, and eventually I did, when I was 17. I spent a year there, and it was an incredible experience. It was the first time I had ever left Ireland, and it broadened my horizons to go from my entrenched Northern Irish upbringing, where Catholics lived one end of the town and Protestants the other, to a land where all colours and creeds lived together and nobody ever asked me what religion I was. It was extraordinary to me at the time, and very important, because it made me realise there was a bigger world out there and I longed to be part of it.

My grandparents on my father's side had seven children, all of whom went to their house every Sunday evening, along with their wives, husbands and children. My grandparents' home was a magnet for the entire family. My grandfather, whom we called Granda, had a great big mahogany table, his pride and joy, which he was forever polishing and which dominated the front room. To us children it was vast, and so shiny that we could see our faces in it. It sat in the middle of the living room, with all the chairs pushed back against the walls around it, and all manner of life took place around that table. The children would be drawing pictures down one end, while all the adults would gather round the other end to play cards — whist. We children really felt we'd made it when we were allowed to take a hand. My mother would say, 'Would you just play my hand while I go to the loo, or help out with supper,' and I would glow with pride. The women would be in the kitchen making sandwiches and all kinds of food, the table would be groaning with it, and we'd all eat while the game went on.

Granda was an ex-serviceman who had fought in the First World War, and he lived to the age of 96. (He swore it was the tot of Irish whiskey he enjoyed every night that kept him going.) My grandmother, who was known as Granny Hunniford, was the softest, sweetest, most gentle woman, the epitome of what a granny should look like, with her long grey hair tied up in a bun. She had a small stroke at one point and it gave her a little crooked smile. She was quiet and petite and very beautiful, in her own special way.

A sound engineer I once worked with at the BBC alarmed me by telling me he had the gift of second sight and could see a spirit following me wherever I went. It first of all slightly freaked me out, but when I challenged him to tell me more he described Granny Hunniford in perfect detail, including that special smile, and said she was there to protect me. Suddenly all my unease disappeared; I felt very warmed to think of that, and I still find it most comforting.

As a very headstrong child I had run away from home a few times over the years and I always went to my Granny Hunniford's. She lived about three-quarters of a mile away, so I could walk there, and she would calm me down, make me tea and tell me to get in touch with Mum and let her know where I was. Not that I needed to; my mother always knew where to find me anyway.

Grandparents were absolutely integral to our family structure. I felt I had three homes, Granny McCann's, Granny and Granda Hunniford's and the one where I lived with Mum and Dad.

That's how I wanted it to be for my grandchildren. Right from birth they always spent a lot of time at my home, I kept their toys and bits and pieces there and they knew it was their home, just as much as it was mine. That is still true today, though as teenagers they don't need me to keep toys any more — although I've hung on to a few just for the memories and occasionally that big box of Lego comes out for all to enjoy!

My parents also taught me a lot about how to try to be a good grandparent, when I watched them with my own children. My mother adored Caron from the first moment. She already had a grandson, my sister's son, Lawrence, but she couldn't wait to get her hands on her first granddaughter. In fact at times it was all I could do to prise her off Caron and let me take her home!

When my children were young we lived in Lisburn, a few miles from Belfast. Later we got a bit posher and moved to Hillsborough, which is about 14 miles from Belfast and is where the Queen has her Royal Residence, at the castle. It is an exquisite country village and we were surrounded by fields — I've always loved having the countryside close. Our first house was next to a farm where Paul had a good pal in the farmer's son, in fact at times he almost lived there. It was total escapism — what boy wouldn't relish the big hay sheds to play in, and all the animals. And when he practised on his trumpet, out of the side window of our house, all the cows would come over from the field to listen. It was a hilarious sight — Paul playing away and about 40 cows standing around under the window. As he said, 'The best audience I ever had.'

My parents were a half-hour drive away and I took the children to see them every week. When my babies first arrived I couldn't wait to show them off to my parents. In a way I was so proud of myself for producing them. I really under-stood how devastated Caron felt when her father died just before Gabriel was born; she had been looking forward so much to introducing them and it was a harrowing blow.

Caron had a lovely relationship with my parents. They used to keep her overnight whenever Don and I were away. My mother would say to us, 'You go off and have a nice weekend,' and I knew she and Dad were going to have a whale of a time spoiling Caron.

My mother was a large, jolly woman with a very open face. She laughed easily and loved a good joke; I used to save up all my naughty jokes to tell her. She cooked and baked constantly and would bring all kinds of delicious goodies out of the oven, while my father would make furniture for Caron's dolls' house and other toys. He was very talented and could paint, draw and write poems as well as being incredibly practical.

It was bliss for Caron being with them, and she adored them. My mother gave her an enveloping, cosseted feeling from the start; there was no central heating, so she made cosy hot water bottles and there were warm blankets and flannelette sheets on the big squidgy bed.

Caron was a bonny child, with a shiny rosy-cheeked face. My father used to bring her back to our house on the bus as he worked near to where we lived. When she was a year and a half old, she could sing 'I'll Never Find Another You' by The Seekers, all the way through. Dad used to purposely sit in the front seat of the bus and would coax Caron to stand up, turn around and entertain the entire bus.

When she grew up, Caron couldn't believe she used to do that, but Dad encouraged her — he was as proud as a peacock. They had a very special relationship; there are lots of pictures of Caron in her grandad's arms, or him chasing her round the garden. He was 70 when he died, and Caron was heartbroken. My mother died of breast cancer a few years later, aged 72, and Caron, Paul and Michael missed both their grandparents terribly. They had always been the back-stop and solid foundation of our family circle.

When Paul was born a year and a half after Caron, I was just as keen to take him along to my parents but they felt they couldn't look after both children overnight. A toddler and a baby

58

Charlie
age 10

Grandad has a pint a day, he's cool and wrinkly, mighty and tall. So I get extra. Small. Will I be as bald as his?

might have been just a bit too much. So if we needed to go away overnight, Paul went to my aunt Myrtle, one of my father's sisters, who was like a second grandmother. Myrtle was a brilliant dressmaker. She was so talented that she should have been working for Balmain. You just had to bring her a picture of a dress out of *Vogue*, and she could make it. She made wonderful dresses for Caron, and for her array of dolls.

By the time Michael was born, eight years after Caron, my broadcasting career had just started, so I needed regular childcare. Help was just around the corner in the shape of a lovely retired couple, called Gilly and Papa, who looked after him while I was working. They would pick Michael up from school and then serve him tea on a beautiful trolley as he watched TV by the fire, using the best china cups. Gilly would say to me, 'Darling, you must never let your standards drop.' Michael went through a phase of refusing to eat anything unless it had hundreds and thousands on it, so there would be a packet of them sitting ready on the tea trolley.

Papa was a retired bank manager and he would talk endlessly to Michael about all sorts of subjects. I always thought Papa enhanced Michael's word skills, because he can talk the hind legs off a donkey, and talk to anyone, no matter who or what they are.

At Christmas and on special occasions we would all go to my parents' house. It was only a two-up, two-down house, but somehow we fitted in Don, me and our three children plus my sister Lena, her husband and their three children, my brother Charles, his wife and their two children as well as my parents — 16 of us in all. Caron and I used to laugh about it and say, 'How did we all fit in?' Goodness knows but we did, and we wouldn't have dreamed of going anywhere else for Christmas. My parents had knocked the wall through to join their two downstairs rooms with an archway and they set out two tables, one for the adults and one for the children, either side of the archway. An enormous amount of fun was had around those tables. It seems, when I look back, that so much of our family life revolved around food and eating, and my children still talk about those simple times with great affection.

When Michael was 10, Paul was 16 and Caron was 18 I moved to England. At that time I was presenting a very successful television show in Northern Ireland, called *Good Evening, Ulster,* with no ambitions whatsoever to move to

London. But out of the blue came an offer from BBC Radio 2 to deputise for Jimmy Young for two weeks while he was on holiday. Moving from Northern Irish politics to international politics was a bit of a shock to the system, but I enjoyed doing the show enormously. At the end of my two weeks all I hoped for was that maybe they would ask me to deputise again on a future occasion, so I was shocked and elated when they offered me my own Radio 2 show. As it turned out, I was to become the first woman to have a daily show on Radio 2, a hugely exciting opportunity that would mean a big jump from provincial to national broadcasting.

It was clearly a major decision to move, and we had a big family discussion about it. But, as Don rightly pointed out, I would have been hell to live with if I hadn't given it a go. Don and I had never been apart for more than 10 consecutive days in 20 years of marriage, but at that time, coincidentally, he also received an exciting offer — six months' work as a television producer in South Africa.

In the end we both accepted the offers we had been made, and we agreed to see how it went. In the ensuing months we found ourselves on very different paths. In my opinion, long separations rarely work and eventually we mutually agreed to make our temporary separation permanent, though we always remained good friends and the family circle stayed strong.

While moving to England offered me an exciting new stage in my career, it also coincided with Caron starting an English and Drama degree at Bristol University and Paul going to the Guildford School of Drama to study stage management. I was delighted that Michael — who was still at primary school — and I would be closer to my two older children, but it was dreadful for my mum, who found it hard to cope with me and the children moving so far away. I promised I would come back to visit her once a month, which I did.

Gradually I began encouraging my mother to come over to England to visit me. At first she wasn't certain, but in the end she agreed and she loved it. My sister Lena, who still lived just up the road from Mum, often came too, and the two of them would have a lot of fun, shopping and going to shows as well as catching up with me and my children.

At that time Des O'Connor had a weekly TV entertainment show, and one Mother's Day he decided to do a special programme, talking to the mothers of some well-known TV chat-show hosts. He invited my mother to go on the show, along with Russell Harty's and Michael Parkinson's mothers.

Mum wasn't sure whether she could or should do it, but my sister, anticipating another shopping trip to London, soon talked her into it. They were flown over, taken to a lovely hotel and then whisked to the studio in a grand limo, where my mother was made up and had her hair done by the expert backstage girls before making her appearance with the other mothers. Michael, Russell and I were told not to come anywhere near the place in case we cramped their style!

Live on air, Des asked the mothers what they thought had made us into chat-show hosts. My mum told Des that he might be surprised to hear I had been tongue-tied as a baby. Tongue-tie is a condition in which the membrane attaching the tongue to the floor of the mouth is extended. It clamps down the end of the tongue and results in an inability to stick out your tongue, in other words limits movement. It runs in our family; my father had it and so did my son Michael. These days the membrane is surgically snipped in hospital, but as my mother told Des, in those days the GP often did it with a pair of silver scissors, and that's what happened in my case.

After telling the story my mother paused, and then with perfect comedic timing added, 'Do you know, Des, I often wonder, did I do the right thing?'

The entire studio collapsed with laughter, Des could barely speak and my mother was an instant hit. In fact she dined out on that appearance for years, speaking about it to local groups like the Women's Institute and enjoying the story all over again.

The day after her appearance on Des's show Caron and I took her to the Ritz for tea. I began going to the Ritz in my early days in London, mainly because, naively, it was one of the few places I knew of and therefore an easy place to suggest meeting someone.

As we led her through to the Palm Court my mother was amazed and a little overwhelmed by the grandeur of the place. We were greeted by the head waiter, a lovely Irishman called

Michael, who had been there for 27 years and who knew both Caron and me very well. He always got the pianist to play 'When Irish Eyes Are Smiling' and made a fuss of us, but on this occasion Caron and I were ignored as he turned to my mother.

'Madam,' he said, bowing low, 'may I say you were sensational on the Des O'Connor Show last night.' My mother beamed at the thought of being recognised in London, as he fussed around her, making sure she had everything she needed. At the end of our visit he brought her a beautiful oval box of Ritz chocolates, adorned with a big froufrou bow, resting on a highly polished silver tray. She was absolutely thrilled with the gesture.

When my mother died and Caron and I went through her things we found those chocolates on the sideboard in her house, still unopened. They had brought her incalculable pleasure.

One Christmas I bought her a little half-jacket in dark mink. She thought it was the most glamorous thing she'd ever seen, and she wore it when I took her to the Royal Variety Show the following year. We got ready at the London Weekend Television studios, where I was working at the time, and when we left the building the security man, whom I knew, made sure she could hear when he turned to me and said, 'Gloria, your mother is one hell of a looker.' My mother was thrilled, and enjoyed a flirt and a joke with him before we went off to the theatre for the big show.

Mum often came over to stay for a week or two, and Caron, Paul and Michael would all come over to Sevenoaks to see her. Caron and I would take her shopping, and on one occasion we all took her on a day-trip to France from Dover, which is close to where I live. Mum bought Limoges china as holiday gifts for all her friends, which we had to pack very carefully for her flight back to Belfast.

My mother was always thrilled to see her grandchildren, and kept in touch with them all the time. She was a good and constant letter writer. My children in turn idolised my parents and wanted to replicate this loving grandparent — grandchild relationship when their own children were born. I believe there is so much to be gained from both sides, when grandparents and their grandchildren are close. And having known what it was to have loving grandparents, I was also very keen to try to provide this same experience for my grandchildren.

It's a very Irish thing, maintaining the traditional family unit, but the Irish are by no means alone in feeling it is special. I have come across families from so many cultures — Jewish, Indian, Arab, Afro-Caribbean, French, Italian, Greek, English, Scottish, Welsh and many, many more — all of whom are keeping the generations of their families closely connected and holding on to family traditions.

Not long ago I was hosting an episode of *Cash in the Attic* when I interviewed a woman who was selling her house because her daughter had persuaded her to buy the house next door to her. The woman still had her own mother, in her nineties, who was moving with her, and the daughter had two little girls. So four generations of the same family would be living in the two houses. I thought that was wonderful.

I have spoken to many others who remember their grandparents with love and affection, even if, in some cases, they appeared a little stern or distant at times. Grandparents in the past tended to be less hands-on, and many didn't play games with their grandchildren as we might now, but they were solid and loving presences who made a huge difference to family life.

Of course there are plenty of first-time grandparents today who have no experience of their own grandparents. And while it's wonderful to have a model of a loving grandparent to follow, you can still be a wonderful grandparent. All it takes is to follow your heart and offer your grandchild love, warmth, kindness and a solid presence they can trust. You can give them no greater gift, and they in turn give you the joy of all the fun and laughter that young people bring to any family.

My Nana

My nana has a hobby of throwing bricks at ducks but wen I go to her house my hobby is eating Nana's home made eclaires and her rost dinner is to diy for and she is vary short so she can't drive.

By Maisie age 11

4

The Early Years

By the time Beau arrived we had four little grandsons under the age of five and on Stephen's side three boys and a girl, so we already had our own seven-a-side football team. And right from the start I saw as much of them as possible.

I wanted to be a good grandmother and I thought a lot about what that would mean. I had the wonderful examples of my own grandparents and my parents, but my circumstances were very different to theirs; like so many other women, I was a modern working grandmother, and that meant some things would be different.

The most important thing, I knew, was to see them as much as possible. You have to make an effort to build a relationship with your grandchildren, nurture the relationships and share as much as possible. And that means being with them; it's that old adage, bonding. I wasn't caring for my grandchildren on a daily basis, as so many grandparents do, because I already had a busy full-on career. So I would visit, and I was very lucky, because both Paul and Caron regularly brought their children to Sevenoaks to see me.

Location plays a significant part in how you build up your relationship with your grand-children, because if they're a long way off and you can't see them more than, say, two or three times a year, then it's very hard to get close, nurture that one-to-one relationship and really know them. If you are lucky enough to have them within reach or even living close by, then savour every minute.

Caron came most often. She regularly came for the weekend, staying over on a Saturday night, with Russ and the children. It became tradition to make Sunday lunch for the whole family, and in a strange way their family unit acted as a nucleus for the rest of the family. Caron would say to her brothers, Paul and Michael, 'You'd better make sure you're there on Sunday.' I loved having them around me and it was an extra bonus when Paul and his family and Michael could make it too.

I obviously love all my grandchildren equally deeply, but I saw more of Caron's boys because she brought them over such a lot. I think daughters tend to gravitate towards their mothers; that's natural and understandable, and we saw each other in London a great deal, when I'd stop off on my way to work. Mothers and daughters are often close; they share confidences and help one another out, both practically and emotionally. Statistics bear this out and show that the mother's mother tends to be 'senior' granny, in the sense that she will be most involved, and most often consulted, so your son's grandchildren are more likely to spend time with their other grandparents.

Caron and I used to talk on the phone, perhaps three or four times a day. She would ring for a quick chat, and because we were in the same business she sometimes wanted to talk about a personality she was going to have on the show, who I might have already interviewed, and compare notes. At other times she would remind me of a date or give me a blow-by-blow account of what the boys were up to. She was so proud of her boys and wanted to share their milestones and achievements. I was privy to their first smiles, words and steps.

Russ, whose parents totally adored the boys, but lived some distance away, was very patient and supportive. I know there were weekends when, after a tough working week, he would probably have preferred to relax at home, but if Caron wanted them all to pile into the car and come over to us, he willingly came. Mind you, I always made a big, cooked Irish breakfast for them on Sunday mornings, which I think Russ appreciated.

Caron also enjoyed the break Stephen and I were able to give her and Russ, by cooking and helping to look after the boys at the weekends. They both worked hard, so on Sundays we'd encourage them to have a lie-in while we washed and dressed, fed and played with first Charlie on his own and then, two and a half years later, Gabriel too.

For me it was sheer pleasure. In the early morning the house was quiet and I had the boys to myself and could enjoy them without the phone ringing or the doorbell going or any other interruptions. That made for a very special time, when we chatted, ate breakfast, played in the garden and, of course, made our tea.

One of the things I wanted to do was to create, or carry on, little family traditions — things my grandsons would remember and smile about when they grew up and looked back on their childhood. And top of the list seemed to be drinking tea together.

Tea has always been very important in our household. I was practically weaned on the stuff. My mother would never have the kettle or the teapot half full; they had to be full, because 'you never know who might drop in', as she used to say. And of course the family all drank endless cups of tea. It's always been my favourite drink.

I still stick to a lot of my mother's traditions so I introduced my four grandsons to the joys of tea very young. When we got up together at six in the morning and went down to the kitchen, Charlie would say, 'Tupatea Nana,' and I'd make him a little cup. He loved our tea sessions so much that I bought him his own little teapot in the shape of a rabbit. I kept it for him and when he came over we'd go and get it and make his tea. Gabriel loved tea even more than Charlie. At a year and a half old he'd go and sit at the table in the gazebo in the garden and wait patiently until I came, when he'd say, 'Tea Nana,' and I had to go off and make it. We bought him an entire little tea-set with china cups and a pot, which came in a small wicker basket lined with gingham. He would spill more than he drank, but he loved the ritual of it and the sense of sharing and togetherness.

Jake and Beau also got their own individual

teapots, and when all four boys had their teapots out it was quite a party. I used to buy crazy fun crockery any time I spotted it, just for these tea parties for example cups, saucers and plates in the colours and shape of Battenberg cake, with its squares of pink and yellow. We even have a wooden tea-house in the garden, which Stephen bought me for a birthday present one year, so that in the winter when it's too cold to have tea in the garden we can carry on our tea parties. Even now, when the boys arrive, the first thing I say is, 'Tea?' and they smile and nod — I think they probably go along with it just to keep me happy.

When my children were small we used to have a 'magic' tea-set that was only brought out if they were ill. It was a miniature fine china set in white with green and pink decorations. There was a little teapot, a tiny milk jug and sugar bowl, and a cup, saucer and plate. Tea would be served alongside tiny squares of toast, to tempt flagging appetites, and it helped cure many childhood sniffles, bumps and bruises. I brought the magic teapot over with me from Ireland, and eventually it went to Caron's home in Cornwall. Today I have it in our family home in France, and it will hopefully be there for future generations of tea-drinkers.

Children today tend to be occupied for a lot of their time with endless activities. They go to all sorts of things after school, many of them extremely worthwhile, like music lessons, cubs, sports clubs and so on. But the result is that their week can be filled with countless things they *have* to do, places they *have* to be and timetables. I wanted their time with us to be a contrast to this, a space in their lives with as few 'musts' as possible, no set routines other than meals and bedtime, and an opportunity for them to get nice and grubby while having fun.

We're lucky enough to have a good-sized garden and the children used to play in it for hours. There's a rather overgrown corner, behind some tall trees, that they called the 'jungle', and I used to listen to them playing imaginary games there. I loved that they were getting the best combination known to man — or perhaps I should say boy: fresh air and imaginations running riot. There were some old paving stones and bricks there and they'd paint things like 'This Way to the Club' or 'Charlie's Cubby' on them. They hung ropes from trees and propped ladders against them and they'd make caves, hideouts and camps, putting up tents in the space under the trees and spending hours in them. They'd explore, fight crocodiles, have sword fights with sticks and hunt tigers — filthy dirty but blissed out!

I'd leave them to it, arriving from time to time with cold drinks, if it was a hot day, or tea if it was cold, plenty of sandwiches and biscuits and goodies so that they could have lunch in their tent. Often I'd crawl in and have it with them. They lived in T-shirts and shorts in the summer days, and they'd come in at the end of the day absolutely exhausted and needing a bath. I loved that; it seemed to me the way little boys should be.

74

It's quite revealing that even when children are in their early teens they still adore having what I call lovely, innocent fun. Recently we went to Cornwall with the boys, where they still relished the simple pleasure of crabbing. They would go to the local fish shop to collect the waste fish heads, attach them to their lines and hey presto — 66 crabs! They were so proud of their catch. Of course they let them all go, and then took photos of 66 crabs moving sideways down the slipway. I always think the same poor crabs get caught over and over again by the legions of children who enjoy crabbing in the summer!

In the evenings we sat up later than we should have, playing hotly competitive games of Scrabble, Perudo and Cheat. At the end of the holiday I realised we had hardly watched any TV and had barely seen a computer all week, and we'd had a great deal of good old-fashioned fun.

Stephen has been a fantastic step-grandfather to the boys and he gave them another special element to their time with us. He's a doer, always busy with his hands, mending or making something, and the boys, of course, loved to join him when he was busy on some repair, decorating job or creation. When he was a toddler Charlie used to say, 'Stevie, can we do fixing now?' and they'd go off together to find some wood to hammer nails into. We got Charlie a little toolbox one Christmas and took him along to choose the tools to go in it. We'd keep it at our house and when it was time to do some 'fixing' he'd run off and get it.

Jake and Gabriel also enjoyed helping

Stephen. But the child who enjoyed 'fixing' the most was, and still is, Beau. He really took to woodwork and making things, and we bought him a great big toolbox which his dad still occasionally digs into. Beau has made all sorts of things including a little table which sits in our garden, and a chair which he took home and painted. One of my favourite photos is of Stephen in a joiner's apron with Beau and his toolbox beside him — the carpenter and his mate.

The other day Paul came by for a cup of tea and asked whether Stephen had a couple of hinges he could take home for Beau, who needed them for something he was making. I had to laugh; instead of sending sweets or goodies over, we were sending hinges. Apparently the first thing Beau said when Paul got home was, 'Dad, did you get the hinges from Stevie?'

One of the things I've always loved best about being a grandmother is the opportunity to spoil them. Not massively, just a bit. (I lie!) Of course I would tell them off if I had to, I don't take any nonsense, but on the whole I don't want to be the disciplinarian, bossing them around. I felt I had done the bossy bit with my own children and I want to be the fun, cuddly nice Nana who has places to go and yummy things to eat. So I always have a goody cupboard in the kitchen, stocked with the biscuits, cakes and sweets they like, and when they were tiny their eyes were like saucers as they watched me delve into it for treats. Both my grandmothers spoiled me rotten, and I loved being able to do that in turn for my grandchildren. Obviously I'm conscious, these days, of not giving them too many sweet things, and I was impressed a few weeks back when I took Beau out for an ice-cream and instead he opted for a bag of pears, bananas and red peppers — he eats peppers like some children eat apples, crunching into them.

It was the former Mayor of New York Rudi Giuliani who said, 'What children need are the essentials that grandparents provide in abundance. They give unconditional love, kindness, patience, humor, comfort, lessons in life. And, most importantly, cookies.' I often felt I had the cookie part sorted, and I was doing my best with the rest!

One of the things I felt most strongly was that I wanted my grandsons to feel that our home, Stephen's and mine, was their second home. I wanted it to be somewhere that was permanent and unchanging, safe and reliable, that they could always return to. This became even more important for Charlie and Gabriel in the years that their mum was ill. And sadly, she became ill such a short time after Gabriel, her second son, was born.

At that point so much changed. The sunny, uncomplicated days we'd enjoyed after Charlie's birth, with everything seemingly in its place, gave way to a very difficult and dark time. Caron was hit by the double emotional upheaval of her father's death and her son's birth at the same time. It floored her, and although it wasn't officially diagnosed we felt pretty certain that she was suffering from postnatal depression, which lasted for the next few months.

Many families encounter this most debilitating of conditions and, in addition to my own experience of it, I have heard from other grandparents just how tough it can be to watch a daughter suffering. Just when a new mother should be enjoying her baby and feeling at the centre of her family's world, she is hit by a depressive illness which leaves her feeling utterly miserable and, at times, unable to cope. As many as one in seven new mothers experience some degree of postnatal depression, so it's pretty common. Most new mums remember the 'baby blues' that time in the few days after giving birth when your hormones are all over the place and you feel a bit weepy.

For the majority this soon passes, while for some women it develops into full-blown depression, with sleep disturbances, low moods, inability to concentrate or function properly and loss of appetite and a sense of failure. Many well-known women have talked openly about going through this experience, for example the broadcaster Fern Britton. She has said that it took her years to sort it out in her head and get it all into perspective, and she's given a graphic account of what she went through:

'I used to fantasise about getting into the car and driving at a wall. It wasn't to kill myself, just to turn off the light, make things stop. It's to stop the noise in your head, the pain in you — you just want it to stop. It's not an indulgence and it's not attention-seeking and it's not being needy — all the accusations I'd had thrown at me. It's none of that. If there had been an option saying 'Do you want to go to sleep for a year?' the answer would have been a resounding 'Yes'.

'I was put on Prozac. I'd had what amounted to a breakdown, but nobody had known because I'd become so adept at hiding it. I'd be privately sobbing, but if someone came into the room I could turn round and go, 'Hi, how are you, let's put the kettle on.''

Caron suffered from all the classic symptoms, but the worst was her inability to sleep. Night after night she lay awake, tossing and turning and unable to find peaceful rest. As anyone who has lost out on sleep for a prolonged period of time knows, there are few things worse. It's crazy-making, you feel exhausted, irritable, emotionally vulnerable and very low.

For me it was very tough to see my bright, energetic and capable daughter turning into someone who struggled to function. I knew she was grieving for her dad, and I desperately wanted to help her, but grief is such an individual thing and it seemed there was little I could do, apart from being there as much as possible for her and the boys and giving her time to talk.

When a parent is struggling to cope, a grandparent can step in. I know that some step in full-time, others dip in and out, trying to get the balance right. As I still worked full-time myself, I went round to Caron and Russ's house as often as I could, and I had the boys for them at weekends whenever they needed me to. I worried that the boys would sense their mum was unwell, and hoped I might be able to give them reassurance by keeping things absolutely normal at my home.

With children things are almost always quite simple, especially when they are very young. They need to eat, sleep, have loads of cuddles, be played with and bathed. And the business of seeing to those things is, in some ways, balm to the soul, because it is so beautifully straightforward.

I have always known, through my own experiences as a child, that grandparents are terribly important. And I think it is in times of trouble — such as illness or divorce — that they are most important of all. Grandparents can provide continuity, calmness, reassurance, tenderness, warm beds, square meals and hot tea!

At one point during this period, when we thought things were settling down, Stephen and I went on holiday to Barbados. It had been planned for a long time, but soon after we arrived Michael phoned and asked us to come back, saying that Caron needed me home. We caught the next available flight, and half an hour after we got to Sevenoaks Russ arrived with Caron.

She looked more unwell than I had ever seen her before. She couldn't walk without Russ's support, she was limp and weak, and there were purplish patches around her mouth, her eyes looked dull and her face expressionless. I was truly shocked, but I knew I mustn't show it, so instead I smiled, kissed her and took her straight upstairs to bed.

For the next few days Stephen and I looked

after Caron. As we were still supposed to be on holiday no-one knew we were back, so I often refer to them as our stolen days. Caron had been on anti-depressants which clearly weren't right for her, and they were partially responsible for the alarming change in her. Once she stopped taking them, and with rest, pampering and good food, she brightened and her strength began to return. We pottered around the garden in the sunshine, I cooked fresh food three times a day, we played cards and Caron read and painted until gradually she recovered.

I hoped the worst was over, and life would get back to normal, but sadly that wasn't the end of her depressive phase. When she went back home she was still unable to sleep and it was some time before things improved. But by the summer after Gabriel's birth, when he was six or seven months old, she seemed much better. She was able to laugh again, she began to sleep properly and we felt we had her back again.

I was hugely relieved, as were the rest of the family. We hoped it had been a blip, and that life could carry on as before, but sadly that wasn't to be the case, as only weeks later Caron was to start her battle with cancer.

In the tough times that followed I wanted to be there for the boys, offering them stability and love. I felt that if other people in their lives, in addition to their parents, offered them unconditional love, then it would help them to feel secure, and to trust that the world was a good place, even if difficult and painful things sometimes happened.

It was also good for them to spend time with their extended family. I love it when my children and grandchildren are all around me, and special days in the calendar — Christmas, birthdays, holidays and celebrations — have always been times when we gather the family together at our home. It was natural that they should all come to us, just as my brother, sister and I all went to our parents. So I would — and still do — encourage everyone to come over to us and put together a mountain of food for us all to share during a noisy meal, full of talk and laughter.

Families have different ways of celebrating and having fun, and for us it has always involved music and songs. I sang on stage from the age of eight, alongside my magician father, doing the circuit of halls, clubs and concerts in Northern Ireland, and all three of my children were very musical. Caron loved to sing as a child, while Paul was a superb drummer and Michael had a brilliant voice, although he was the one who was least extrovert in the singing stakes. I used to put on little 'shows' for our neighbours, charging a penny to get in. My children put them on for us when they were little, and my grandsons have all been just the same.

One of the things I loved was teaching the boys various songs. When I was young and singing with the Mid-Ulster Variety Group, there was one well-known little song we sang at every appearance which started off, 'Here we are again, happy as can be'.

★   ★   ★

Grandad likes tractors,
He talks about them all
the time. He likes sneaking
a beer.

Jason age 11

I taught the boys to sing it when they were very small, and they lapped it up. It's such a cheerful song, and so apt when you've having a get-together. Of course they would pooh-pooh the whole thing today — it's definitely not 'cool'!

Another song Stephen and I taught Charlie and Gabriel, on a long drive down to Cornwall one day, was 'Supercalifragilisticexpialidocious'. It's quite a mouthful for two small boys, they must have been aged three and five or six at the time, but by the time we finished that five-hour journey they could do the chorus and the whole first verse, word-perfect, with all the accompanying gestures. It was to become our party piece.

A couple of years later, in Australia, when Caron turned 40, we helped the boys put together a little surprise 'concert' for her. They were aged five and seven by then, and they rehearsed zealously and sang her both these songs. They even added the second verse of 'Supercalifragilistic'. They rounded it off with 'Happy Birthday to You' and Caron absolutely adored it — her eyes shone with delight.

All four boys loved putting on shows for us in our conservatory, and used to insist that we bought tickets and took our seats in the 'audience'. They're all born entertainers and would sing, dance, play instruments, write their own songs and plan their own announcements and introductions. Caron used to say there was an entertainment by-pass on our side of the family.

One of the funniest phases the family went through was when everyone was crazy about *Riverdance*. Caron loved it, she had the album and took it everywhere with her. At family parties, after a few glasses of wine had been consumed, she and Stephen would slip away and then emerge from behind a pillar or through a doorway, arm in arm, backs stiff as rods, tapping and jumping away. It was hilarious.

The children wanted in on the action, so next time we went to see them we bought them tap shoes and they spent hours playing the *Riverdance* album and tapping their way up and down the long wooden hall of the house in Cornwall where Caron and Russ had moved to by then, in search of a more peaceful life. The children really made us laugh — there was an enormous amount of laughter and many fun times, despite Caron's illness, and I am always glad that we all have so many special memories to look back on.

That's one of the things I think grandparents can do — help create happy memories. Stephen and I used to love dreaming up ways to give the boys a good time or, more importantly, to do something *new* with them. We always put a lot of thought into presents, because most children tend to have a lot of toys, so we tried to find things that might hold a special place in their hearts.

When Charlie was about 18 months old we bought him a battery-operated red jeep for Christmas that he could sit in and zoom around in. He absolutely loved it, and as the other boys came along they all grew to love the red jeep in turn. They raced around the garden in it at a furious rate. How it, and they, survived I'll never know.

By the time Beau was three or four he was so keen on the jeep that he longed for one of his own. So we bought him a blue one. He got lots of Harry Potter gear that Christmas too, because he was mad about the boy wizard. We were in Cornwall for Christmas, as by that time Stephen and I had bought a small house down there to be near Caron in case she needed it, and we will never forget little Beau riding his jeep around Fowey, wearing his witches' hat and Harry Potter specs. It was, to use an apt phrase, magical.

I think all grandparents — or most, anyway — want to be there for their grandchildren and be remembered by them for their humour, warmth, solid presence and love. I always think if you're not sure what to do in any situation, act with love, and it will turn out all right. And if you do get it wrong, at least you know you had the best of intentions.

Our children are really special (although we all say that). We love their company, and we like them as well as love them, and we're hugely proud of them. They're very loving and unrestrained; they still wrap their arms around us when they come, even though they're older now and in the awkward teenage years. That's a very comforting feeling, and I like to think it's because they have always been so loved.

5

Grandparents as Carers

One of the most important jobs grandparents do is care for their grandchildren while parents are at work. During the credit crunch many families have found it hard to get by and cope with financial cuts and both parents simply have to work.

Huge numbers of grandparents do this — around one in four of the 14 million grandparents in Britain — which means there are three and a half million grandparents caring for grandchildren on a regular basis. As the vast majority do this work unpaid, they are also making a big contribution to the economy — the childcare that grandparents provide was recently valued at just under £4 billion a year.

A report that came out in August 2010 said that grandparents are now more vital to families' basic childcare routines than ever before. Half of all couples now rely on grandparents in order for both of them to go back to work after the birth of a child, and this figure is even higher for single parents. Parents need to work, and many simply don't earn enough to be able to pay childminders — childcare costs in Britain are the highest in Europe.

However, while financial necessity is a huge factor, there's more to it than just that: parents want their children to be with people who are safe and familiar and who love them. In so many cases no-one can fill that role better than grandparents.

I have never been one of the grandparents who is able to offer regular daily childcare, because I have a full-on and demanding job which I love and want to do. Interestingly, the British Social Attitudes survey indicates that 63 per cent of grandmothers under the age of 60, with a grandchild under age 13, are working, so I know I'm by no means alone.

Of course there have been plenty of times when Paul or Caron would say 'Can you have the kids?' and I'd do my best to say yes, even if that meant moving things around a bit. But I couldn't do it week in week out at a fixed time. In some ways I feel sad about that, because time with our grandchildren has always been so precious, and I would have loved more of it. The one time I did look after my grandchildren, day to day, was when Caron and Russ were in Australia. They moved there for just over two years, as Caron felt it was a healthier environment to deal with her cancer. Stephen and I went out to see them eight times, often staying for weeks or even months at a time. During those periods we became the backup mechanism for Caron and Russ, doing the school runs, cooking and spending time with the boys. I felt extremely close to Charlie and Gabriel at that stage, and I went to Australia as much for them as for Caron.

I've talked to lots of parents and grandparents,

and I admire and respect those grandparents who offer childcare, because it can be hard work and can sometimes feel rather thankless. Much of what I've learned is borne out by the research that has been done on this area. Parents want grandparents to look after their children, but they can also get annoyed and frustrated when grandparents don't stick to their rules around discipline and care. And on the other hand, grandparents can end up feeling taken for granted and unappreciated. So it can be a bit of a minefield!

Most grandparents who help with childcare don't have the children full-time. A lot offer one, two or three days a week; the average is just under 16 hours, or two full working days. This is often because the grandparents are still working themselves, and that's all they can manage — now that there is no official retirement age many will carry on working, through either choice or necessity. But in some cases it's because, while grandparents want to help, they don't want their lives to be taken over by childcare.

Take Dianne, who is 62 and a magistrate. 'I have my two grandchildren every Tuesday, while my daughter is studying to be a psychotherapist. I also babysit on other occasions, but Tuesdays are my regular time with them. I have a grandson of four and a granddaughter of three and I really enjoy them.

'I don't get paid for childcare, and actually I would hate to be paid, but I also wouldn't want to care for the children full-time. That would be like being the mother of small children again, and I've done that once already!

'I actually enjoy my grandchildren more than I enjoyed being a mother. I was very alone and isolated as a young mother, my husband was away working a lot and I found the relentlessness of it hard. So it's lovely being with my grandchildren, and also to be able to hand them back.

'I'm a slightly naughty grandmother, the kind who will sneak the children an ice-cream behind their mother's back. She's the kind of mother who will only give them tuna once a week because of the risks, and I admire her for it, but I like being able to break the rules.'

Rules can definitely be a bone of contention. Parents want grandparents to do it their way, naturally, while grandparents don't always want to be told how to do things, especially when the parents aren't around. So it was lovely to talk to a grandmother I know, Jane, whose daughter is very supportive.

'I have my little granddaughter twice a week. She's 16 months and a sweetheart, though it's hard work and I'm exhausted by the time she goes home. I'm 66 and it can be tough running around after her. My daughter's a teacher and she and her husband are short of money, so I wouldn't dream of asking them for any; I'm glad to help out.

'When I first started looking after India my daughter said to me, 'You discipline her just the way you did when you brought me up.' I was touched by that, it was a generous things to say, and must mean my daughter thinks I got some things right!'

92

That kind of generosity seems to be fairly rare: mostly parents have their own rules and they're not always the same as the ones they grew up with. So what do you do if a potential conflict or resentment is brewing away under the surface?

Based on the conversations I've had with so many parents and grandparents in this position, and advice from the people running some of the wonderful organisations and websites in existence now, including the Grandparents' Association, I've come up with a suggested list of do's and don'ts for grandparents thinking of taking on childcare, or for those already doing it, who aren't completely happy with the way things are working.

In the first place, you need to think about whether you really want, and are willing, to take on regular childcare. It's absolutely fine for parents to ask, but that doesn't mean you automatically have to say, 'Yes.' In fact it's crucial that you only agree if it feels right and possible and you want to do it. Interestingly, a lot of mums and dads say that if grandparents occasionally say no they feel better, because they know that when those same grandparents say yes they really mean it.

I once asked glamorous movie star Lauren Bacall, in an interview, how she enjoyed being a grandmother. She said, 'I adore it, but I pointed out to my children, I loooove my grandchildren, but hey, I'm not becoming a babysitter because I've done that already, with you.'

My friend Jo was equally clear that she didn't want to commit to regular childcare.

'I don't have a formal or regular childcaring commitment,' Jo says. 'I didn't want that. I wanted

93

to keep my freedom. But because my son and his wife work full-time we do look after their two children in the school holidays and I am always happy to fill in, in an emergency. And we babysit, of course, when they need us to. My daughter also lives close to us, with her two children, but she and my daughter-in-law are very good, they never impose on us, they say I have done my bit already by bringing up four children!'

Of course it can be tricky if the parents just appear to assume you will be doing the childcare. If this seems to be the case, then the sooner you say something, the better. Any assumptions need to be brought out into the open and discussed.

But before you can have that discussion you need to decide whether you are going to offer childcare or not, and if so, how much. Will it fit in with your work, and the other pressures and demands of your week? Some grandparents are still caring for their own elderly parents and can feel sandwiched in between the generations, with their own needs completely lost or ignored. But you can't expect people to recognise your needs if you don't tell them. So it really is all right to say, 'Actually, I don't think I can fit that in,' or 'I can do one day a week, but two would be too much, because I need a little time for myself.' It's not wrong, especially when you've worked hard all your life and you want some of that freedom and flexibility that you've been looking forward to.

I do understand how hard it can be to speak up — or to give yourself time, for that matter. I'm pretty hopeless on that front myself, with my

Ulster work ethic; I'll look for an oven to clean, a letter to answer or a phone-call to make before I'll sit down with a cup of tea and put my feet up. But I'm learning, if only because you simply can't go at 100 miles an hour forever, and I'm discovering, as so many of us do, that the world won't stop just because I relax for 10 minutes.

So think about what you need before you agree to take on regular childcare. In fact the best piece of advice I heard was to say to the parents, when they ask, 'Can I think about that and get back to you?' Then take a day, maybe a couple, to be honest with yourself about what you feel able to give and can actually manage.

Joanna is a busy working grandmother but she agreed to spend half a day a week looking after her baby granddaughter Meg, while her daughter-in-law had a much-needed afternoon to herself to shop, clean, have a bath or just catch up with a friend.

'My son and I had to negotiate,' Joanna says. 'I held back a bit at first, when Meg was born — I didn't want to get in the way. But my son phoned me and said what kind of granny was I and that I wasn't involved enough. He was very direct, but we've always been direct with one another, and although it was a difficult conversation I'm so glad we had it. Although I realised that my son wanted me to be involved, I had felt very sensitive since my husband's death and didn't want to appear needy or dependent on them.

'I work full-time, in publishing, so I had to think hard about what I could change and how

95

much time I could give. My son wanted me to do a day, but I felt that half a day was enough, at least for the moment. I had to reorganise work a bit, but now I love my half day with Meg, who is 17 months old. I'm so glad to have that time with her and to see her change and grow.'

Jim and his wife Lisa look after their three-year-old granddaughter Mattie for one day a week.

'Mattie is at nursery three days a week, so we have her one day and her other grandparents do the other day,' he says. 'That works out fine, we love to see her, but more than a day a week would feel too much because she keeps us busy! There are plenty of us granddads doing childcare. The other day I was trying to sort out a day to meet a friend and he said, 'How about Thursday?'

'I said. 'No, I can't do that, it's granddaughter day.'

' 'Oh yes, mine's Tuesday,' he said.

'So you see we're all at it!'

There are certainly more grandfathers than ever getting involved in childcare, and loving it.

'Being a grandfather is the opportunity to see my grandchild develop — crawl, walk, talk for the first time — all things I didn't see with my own child because I was busy working, building a career and a home, and when I got home my daughter was in bed. That's the penalty you pay, but now I can relive those moments through my grandchild,' Jim says.

I always feel touched when I hear how much some grandfathers enjoy their grandchildren, and regret not being there for their own children. In the past men seldom got involved in childcare; it was considered women's work. My dad was really good with children, but he would never have dreamt of changing a nappy. Many women assumed men wouldn't want to get involved, but now we know how far from the truth that is; most men love to get close to their children and grandchildren.

Once you've established the basics of what you are prepared to do, it's a good idea to sit down with the parents — both of them, if they are both around — and discuss the details. This includes the hours, the location — my place or yours — who will drop off or pick up, and so on. After that, discuss the kind of things you're going to do with the child, or children, and what the parents' rules are.

When it comes to a battle of rules, parents come first. If they don't want their child to eat sugar, or watch TV in the afternoon, or have a nap, then it's better to respect that and try to stick to it. However, you can have your say too, especially if the childcare is taking place in your home. You might want a rule such as, no eating in front of the TV, or no feet on the sofa, or shoes off at the front door, and it's right that both children and parents respect that.

One important thing makes a difference here: children are perfectly fine with different rules in different places. They can understand that at granny's they always eat at the table, while at home they can eat in front of the TV, or vice versa. As long as you, and the parents, are clear with them, that's fine. Of course you don't want two entirely different sets of rules, but it's fine to

97

have a few. And that way you feel your voice and your way of doing things matter, and are respected.

I'm a real stickler for eating meals round the table, all together, with no phones or computer games or other gadgets in evidence. I hate all those things, and feel they spoil the meal and allow children to disrespect everyone else at the table and especially the person who has cooked. Parents aren't above getting out their phones at the table sometimes, too! So I just make it a rule, and everyone in my family knows it, and keeps to it. Even some adults can be so rude, texting or receiving texts at the dinner table, so I cheered when David Cameron struck a blow for gadget-free times when he banned all phones in government meetings.

★ ★ ★

There's one important issue that parents and grandparents need to address together, and that's safety, particularly in young children. This probably causes more family worries than all other aspects of childcare put together. Parents are, on the whole, incredibly safety conscious, and grandparents can be even more so. I worried more about having my grandchildren on my own than I did when I was a young mum with children of my own. I took as much care as possible — I was almost paranoid at times, concerned that if anything happened, the parents might think that I hadn't been paying enough attention. The responsibility can be enormous.

There are times, of course, when grandparents

can feel that parents are being a bit over-cautious and should relax more. But on the whole it's better to err on the side of caution when it comes to keeping children safe.

We grandparents tend to argue that we kept all our own children safe, and therefore know perfectly well what we're doing. But hang on a moment — not only was it some time ago that we dealt with children's safety on a daily basis, but we did it in a far more relaxed and easygoing world. Today life is different. No longer can children safely run to the shop around the corner, as we did when I was small, or play outside all day on their own. Then it seemed safe, but now there are more dangers in and outside the home, life is speedier and new hazards have been identified that we have to deal with, so things we thought were fine aren't any longer.

When it comes to safety, check your home thoroughly before grandchildren arrive and remove all obvious hazards, and then follow safety rules while looking after the children. Little things, like never leaving them alone in the bath, emptying the bathwater straight away after the bath and putting in stairgates, will give everyone peace of mind and show the parents that you're taking safety seriously and aren't too proud to listen to advice.

I certainly remember checking around the house for potential hazards when my grandsons got old enough to crawl and then walk. I would have felt so awful if they got hold of anything that hurt them. I personally don't agree with removing every last ornament, however. I taught

99

my own children to respect things in the house, and I have done that with my grandchildren too.

But when it comes to serious hazards, like windows, I am ultra-careful.

Sue tells the story of her small grandson's near-disaster with an open window, and it gives me chills every time I hear it.

'My grandson was two and a half when he came to visit with his mum. It was summer and the window in the bedroom was open a few inches to air the room — something I did every day and which was fine when there were only adults in the house. My daughter-in-law and I were chatting in the kitchen when we realised my grandson had disappeared. I got upstairs just in time to find him hanging out of the window, having climbed up on a stool. I literally grabbed his legs to stop him falling out. It was a heartstopping moment.'

What Sue's story illustrates so well is that when we don't have children in the house we do things and use materials every day that could prove dangerous to a child. So when small children re-enter our lives, and our homes, we have to look at everything with fresh eyes and make sure we're doing all we can to keep children safe.

Once the basic agreement is in place and the safety aspect has been addressed, it's time to tackle one of the trickier aspects of childcare, and that is money. Few grandparents expect to be paid, and few parents can even afford to pay, though they might try to return the favour in kind, with a bit of gardening, perhaps, or an invitation to come on holiday. But while hardly any grandparent expects an hourly rate for the job, there are costs involved, and it must be agreed in advance, if possible, who is going to meet these. There may be bus fares, petrol, there will certainly be food, and there may be nappies or clothing.

Most grandparents who are going to do the childcare in their own homes want to have all the necessary clothes, nappies and food to hand. It's a good idea to stock up on whatever the child will need — perhaps a buggy or a cot, and so on. They needn't be exorbitant; cots, buggies and high-chairs can all be secondhand. Most grandparents are happy to buy the toys and fun things — grandparents spend an average £750 a year, per family, on treats and presents for their grandchildren. That's a fair bit, when many are on low incomes. So if grandparents foot the bill for treats, it's great when parents can pay for the essentials involved in childcare, and perhaps show their appreciation with the odd box of chocolates, a big hug or even a good old-fashioned 'thankyou'. That way grandparents are less likely to feel taken for granted. And a great many do feel taken for granted, sadly.

It's harder to sort out problems when the arrangement is already in place, but it's still important to speak up if something isn't working. One of those who did, and who was glad she did, is Stephanie.

'I was looking after my two little granddaughters three days a week,' she says. 'I'm 63 and I still work two days a week in a supermarket. I'm on my feet all day, and it's pretty tiring.

Spending the other three days looking after a two year old and a four year old left me so exhausted I'd spend the weekend recovering. And it was costing me quite a bit too, in meals, bus fares to the park and so on.

SAFETY CHECKLIST

* Lock away all poisons — medicines and cleaning materials
* Switch off machines like toaster, tumble-dryer and washing machine at the wall
* Protect empty sockets with plastic covers
* Put in gates at top and bottom of stairs
* Put bathroom locks high on the door, out of reach of small people
* Put away keys — don't leave any in the doors or children may lock themselves into rooms, or (as my daughter did) lose all the keys. We never found them and it cost a fortune in locksmiths!
* Make sure the front door is bolted or the safety catch is on
* Cover all fires
* Put away glasses, vases, plants and items than can easily be knocked off shelves, and if you're worried about anything precious, put it out of reach
* Put catches on windows
* If a cupboard or dresser is full of break-ables, make sure it can't be opened

'My daughter Sophie is lovely, but she's a strong character, and I had to think hard before confronting her. In the end I said that while I loved the girls and was happy to have them, I needed to cut back to just two days a week. I said I would give my daughter as much notice as she needed to find an alternative.

'Sophie took it far better than I expected. She said she understood, and six weeks later she told me she had found a reasonably priced childminder who could have them for a day a week. I've got Fridays to myself now, which means I'm not so tired at the weekends and my social life has picked up. The girls are fine with the childminder and I really look forward to having them on the other two days.'

THREE STEPS TO TROUBLE-FREE CHILDCARE

1 *Decide whether you want to offer child-care and if so, how many hours or days a week. Be clear about this with the parents.*
2 *Sort out, in advance, the details such as where you look after the children and who will drop them off or pick them up and at what times.*
3 *Sort out finances; if possible the parents should pay for the child's necessary costs, such as special food or nappies.*

There has been a good outcome all round, but I know it's not always that straightforward. Still, I think a lot of people fear speaking up, and are afraid of rocking the boat, when actually the situation could be resolved. It's often just about *how* you word it. If you can avoid complaining or accusing, and stick to being firm but at the same time friendly, then you're more likely to get your message across.

If you need a bit of extra backup or information the advice and information website www.beGrand.net has a childcare agreement which is simple and straightforward. You can download it and use it as it stands, or simply use it for reference, to remind you of the kinds of areas you need to discuss and be clear about.

You can also look for the ground rules at www.grannynet.co.uk, which take you through the key things you need to discuss before the childcare arrangement begins.

And while the State does very little for grandparents, it's worth noting that from 11 April 2011 working-age grandparents who provide care for a child under twelve will be able to get their National Insurance contributions credited, to help build up their basic state pension.

It's not a lot, but it's a start!

A lot of young parents simply don't know how hard it can be for grandparents to take on childcare. They have busy lives and don't think that perhaps you need a bit of time to yourself. They may see you as the answer to their problems, and forget to consider your needs.

After all, good old mum and dad have always been there and done everything for them. This is far more likely to be because they're being a bit thoughtless than because they don't care. But either way, it's up to you to put them straight. Grandparents shouldn't have to feel guilty, or under pressure to give childcare; it should be part of a loving exchange.

Occasionally I have come across a grandparent who feels a great deal of emotional pressure to offer childcare, when this is something they really feel unable to do. Or in some cases the parent pressures the grandparent to offer more childcare than the grandparent feels able or willing to offer.

One grandmother I spoke to felt deeply upset because her son-in-law threatened to stop her seeing her grandchildren if she didn't agree to his demands. This is totally unacceptable, and it is vital the grandparent stand up for him or herself in such a situation. You can't give in to emotional blackmail or threats of any kind, so stay clear, firm and friendly, while letting parents know exactly what you will and won't do. In most cases idle threats are not followed through.

For the vast majority, things are thankfully simpler. Grandparents are willing to help, and even if it's difficult to agree on the details, most parents would far rather their own parents were looking after the children than anyone else. You're their first choice, and that gives you a bit of bargaining power, especially if you do it with warmth, kindness and a bit of humour.

Generally grandparents will only be asked to

look after preschool age children for the whole working day. Once they're at school it gets easier, because grandparents will probably only be asked to drop them off at school in the morning and pick them up afterwards, and then perhaps look after them for a couple of hours, until mum or dad gets home. It gets more complicated if the parent is doing shift work which involves evenings or weekends, but in the majority of cases, once the grandchildren are at school, the childcare hours are reduced.

'Childcare is a lot simpler since my two grandsons started school,' says Jilly, a grand-mother of 59. 'I looked after them both three days a week until they started school, and I was glad to do it, even though it was pretty full-on. Once the eldest started school two years ago it was much easier, and now that they're both at school I just do an hour before school and three hours after school. My son comes to collect them when he finishes work and rings me if he's going to be late. I have a lovely relationship with the boys, and now that I have them for a shorter time I feel I can enjoy them more, and have fun with them.'

In the end, regular childcare arrangements will only work if both sides are happy — it has to be a win-win situation — so it's worth speaking up, doing a bit of negotiating, being honest and sorting out the details, to get it right.

And while not all grandparents want or are able to take on regular childcare, a huge majority do have their grandchildren to stay, occasionally and sometimes often. And while most look forward to it immensely, they almost universally agree that it's much easier when the parents aren't around! That way grandparents and grandchildren just get on with it, and form their own relationship, without well-meaning parents interfering.

My Grandma

My Grandma hates it when cows walk along the road — especially when they do a plop in the road and she has to drive through it!

Emily
age eleven

mooo

6

Zip That Lip

One of the most sensitive areas grandparents have to manage is whether or not to offer advice and voice your opinion on the way parents are doing things with your grandchildren. This can be a huge learning curve. Sometimes you just can't help yourself — it's on the tongue and then into the brain.

Do you speak up when you feel mothers and fathers are making a meal of something that should be simple, or disciplining their children too much? Do you mention that in your day there wasn't as much junk food, or bedtime was considerably earlier? Do you say something when your daughter is exhausted coping as a new mum and decides that instead of having a much-needed rest she ought to vacuum the house?

These are incredibly delicate areas; it's a real skill to speak up without sounding as though you're being patronising or criticising. Criticism is the last thing a parent, especially a new parent, needs, and if they feel criticised they will probably get angry and defensive and ultimately your relationship with them will change. Bossy grandparents are a bit of a no-no and tend to see less of their grandchildren than those who manage to navigate the delicate path of advice-giving with more sensitivity.

On the other hand, you can't always keep quiet. There are times when giving advice is appropriate and even necessary. So how do you know when to speak up and when to zip your lip? And if you do speak up, how do you say what you want to say in a friendly, supportive way, without being confrontational or critical?

First of all, it helps to remember what it was like for us when we were new parents. Having a baby is a huge, life-changing event. It turns your life and your emotions inside out. Suddenly there's this tiny creature, utterly dependent on you, and for whom you feel a tidal wave of love. But alongside the extraordinary joy of falling in love with your baby there is a minefield to negotiate. How do you care for this little person? Will I be a good parent? What do they need? Are you going to manage all right? Will you ever manage to get enough sleep and get back to work and feel some semblance of routine and normality again?

At a time like this it's both wonderful and daunting to have your parents there. Wonderful because it's so good to feel there is the backup of experience and the insight of people who've been through it all before. And daunting because you feel a tiny bit afraid that they might be judging you and finding your efforts aren't up to scratch.

I can categorically say that I only truly appreciated my parents the second I had my first baby. Only then did I realise why my mum was so concerned about me being out at night, being with the right people, or why she worried about me when I was ill or when I went off to Canada on my own at just 17. It all fell into place with Caron's birth.

She was born when I was on a trip to England, and as she was a month early I didn't fly back to Northern Ireland for a few weeks. During that time I stayed with friends and, kind as they were, they weren't the same as having my family around me, and I felt very lonely. I adored and idolised my baby, but there was no-one to help or advise me, or to really share worries or the joy of my first baby, and I longed for my mother.

When I did finally fly home with my baby, I couldn't wait to show her off to my parents.

With my second and third children, Paul and Michael, it was easier. Not only was I at home, but I had done it all before and caring for a baby didn't seem to be nearly so daunting. When Paul was born and Caron was only 18 months old my parents were marvellous, because they looked after her while I was in hospital and had her over often during those first few weeks, so that I could concentrate on the new baby. I knew my parents were good and loving people, so I was happy to hand my children over to their care. The only funny wrangles we ever had were over food — my mother absolutely refused to cook the children 'new-fangled' foods as she called them, such as spaghetti and rice, preferring to stick to the meat and two veg she had always cooked.

She did, however, give me very constructive comments about how a first child can get jealous of a new baby and how to include Caron and make sure she was part of the whole thing. As it turned out, she loved him so much that Paul became her new doll.

As the children were growing up, my parents proved to be very good indeed at offering support and encouragement while holding back on the criticism. Of course there was the odd time when I felt my hackles rise, but it wasn't often, and for the most part I felt they were behind me in everything I did and I was grateful.

Looking back I can see that my mother must have felt I was doing things very differently from her, because I was a working mother and she had always been at home. But she was never disapproving or judgemental — quite the opposite, she did everything she could to support me.

When the time came for my own children to become parents, I tried to be the same: there to offer advice and help if they needed it, but happy to let them do things their own way, and to offer all the support they needed.

It's only when you become a grandparent that you realise how much parenting changes through the years. Suddenly you realise that all the things you were used to have disappeared. While we used terry nappies and puréed food for our babies, parents today can use disposables and many buy ready-made baby food. Not only that, but all kinds of things go in and out of style. Playpens were once considered very handy, but now they're the equivalent of baby-jail. We used to believe that children should be in a very set routine for feeding and sleeping, but many parents now feed on demand and don't want a rigid routine. Most babies used to be swaddled; parents believed it made babies feel safe and contained; now that's far too restrictive. And while putting babies to sleep on their backs used to be a no-no, it has turned out to be the safest position. We lived by Dr Spock. This book on childcare was our bible in the 60s and 70s, then 20 years later there was total surprise when he said he'd got it all wrong!

The point is, things change all the time, and sometimes we grandparents really don't know best, even though we think we do. We need to learn about how things are done now, much of it based on a great deal of sound research, and be willing to adapt. No-one should be too fixed or rigid in their outlook. And if you are willing to say, 'Do you know, I think the way you're doing that is a whole lot better than what we used to do,' then a new parent is so much more likely to relax and want your advice on a different topic, and you get them on your side. Let's face it, so much depends on the characteristics and personality of the child — they are definately all different.

When Caron, and later Paul, became parents, I did my best to do things the way they wanted them to be done, rather than imposing my own views. And so when from time to time they did ask my advice, I was secretly delighted. I always felt I came into my own when it came to school choices — Caron used to ask me to come along and have a look and tell her and Russ what I thought. And when the children were sick or feverish, Caron would be on the phone asking

113

me what I thought she should do.

One of the things that has really changed since I became a mum is how hands-on many dads are now. My first husband Don didn't change his ways at all when our children came along, it was just expected that I would look after them, and although he loved them very much, he carried on with his life just as it had been before and just as my dad had done. In macho Ireland a man would never ever have wheeled a pram down the street; it was regarded as too sissy. Jobs in those days were easily divided and defined; my mum did all the home-making and childrearing and my dad went out to work and then did all the blokish things like DIY and maintenance. The dividing line was so strict that my mum only ever went out in the evening if it suited my dad to babysit. Strangely she always seemed to accept that that was just the way it was.

Meanwhile Don carried on playing golf on Saturdays and Sundays, leaving me to care for and entertain the children. My children have since asked me how I put up with their dad being away working all week and out for most of the weekend. I did because it was that macho Irish thing again. However, the upside is that the kids still remember Saturday afternoons when their dad was at golf and we all curled up to watch a movie by the fire, with a big chocolate roulade to share.

In contrast my son-in-law Russ was involved with his children right from the start. He was lucky in that he ran his own business and so had some flexibility in his working hours, and he spent all the time he could with Charlie and Gabriel, doing everything for them that their mum did. Paul was the same when his sons arrived; he took on his share of changing, feeding and cuddling and as a result had a warm, close and deeply connected relationship with them from the start.

I love watching these modern, adept fathers, and I feel a little sad for dads who in the past, because of convention, missed out on that loving bond from the beginning with their children. There's no doubt in my mind as I get older that those one-to-one experiences and outings with parents stand out as the halcyon moments.

For me the special time was Saturday morning, when my dad and I set off on our bikes into Portadown, our local town, and went to the ice-cream shop where I would have a pineapple ice-cream delight in a dish. That was one of the best moments in my week, not just because of the ice-cream, but because I had my dad to myself.

As the children got older I recognised that there were a lot of things about modern parenting that were so much better than the way we did it. I love the way parents listen to their children's feelings so much more readily now. In the past children's feelings were not always considered; the 'speak when spoken to' ethos was predominant and the thoughtful, caring concern that many adults show now for children's feelings and wishes was largely absent. When I was young we had to accept our parents' word because 'I say so' certainly reigned supreme. My dad's word was law. The good side of this was that adults got to have conversations without children interrupting, but the downside was that we children were not often listened to.

On the other hand, I think many modern parents explain a bit too much. Sometimes you really do need to say 'because I say so' when asking a child to do something, rather than giving a long explanation of exactly why it must be done. Some children soon latch onto this and ask endless questions, just to put off having to do whatever the chore is. A clever friend of mine deals with it like this:

Mum: 'Go and tidy your room.'

Child: 'Why do I have to?'

Mum: 'I'll tell you why, after you've done it.'

Of course the child knows why she has to tidy her room; she's just playing for time. Offering to give the explanation *after* the chore is done works wonders. It's not often that the child comes back and says, 'I've done it, now tell me why I had to do it.'

I was highly amused recently to see novelist, former Junior Health Minister and now grandmother Edwina Currie on television recently, advocating that children should be trained just like dogs. That sounds a little extreme, but I have to admit within her rant she had some good points. She said that very young children need clear instructions, just like very young pups. Until children develop the power of reasoning, they simply have to learn to obey, and accept that 'rules are rules' in order for us to keep them safe. Edwina said she had always operated on

116

this principle, and now her daughter was bringing her own child up in the same way.

One of the examples Edwina mentioned was that one day she came out of her house to find her neighbour standing beside the car, looking very forlorn and holding her two-year-old granddaughter by the hand. When Edwina asked what was wrong, the neighbour said, 'She won't get into the car; if I try to put her in, she cries.'

Edwina replied, 'So she cries — she's two!'

We have all discovered, in our experience, that at times there is absolutely no reasoning with a two year old. A toddler needs to know exactly what is what and who is in charge.

It's when a child grows a little older that you can begin to explain things, and to help them understand the world around them and the decisions that adults make.

One very poignant scene in our family always sticks in my mind. Caron and Russ had gone to Australia, in the hope of helping her health, and after three months they decided they would stay on and live there for a while.

They made the decision around Easter 2001 when Stephen and I had gone out for the first of our many visits. And after telling us, Caron sat down with Charlie, then aged seven, to tell him.

Charlie was distraught. He wanted to go back to Cornwall, where they had been living for the past year, to see his friends. He ran upstairs crying and shouting, 'I don't want to stay here; I want to go back to Cornwall!'

Caron asked me to go and calm him down, so I went up and cuddled him. I really understood how he felt; it was terrible for me too, and I wanted to say, 'I feel exactly like you.'

When he'd stopped crying I brought him back down, and Caron spoke to him again. Looking him straight in the eyes, she said, 'You have to trust us as parents that this is the best decision for us as a family at this time. It's hard to understand now, but you will one day. And when you're older you can make your own decisions.'

I thought that was a really good way of putting it and negotiating with a child. She acknowledged his feelings, but made it clear that the parents were in charge and he would have to accept it. And he did. Sometimes parents just have to be parents.

Children today are encouraged to think for themselves from an early age — something I really like. And as a result they're not afraid to speak up, and often have their own rationale, which can lead to some very interesting and amusing conversations. I think they feel more confident and they certainly know that they have rights and entitlements. Again, I think this is a good thing — children are little people, with all the big feelings, fears, hopes and needs just like the rest of us. A hundred years ago children were given orders and expected to put up with whatever adults decided, without consultation and generally with very little consideration. When I think how much has changed in just a few generations, I feel like cheering.

Wonderful as the changing attitude to children is, there is a downside, in that so much revolves around children that it can be quite hard to have

My grandad loves
his golf and walking
Sam aged 10

My Nana talks when we watch
T.V, but it dosen't matter.
Sam aged 0

By Sam Boyle

a conversation without a little voice interrupting in the middle. When I was small, children really did only speak when they were spoken to. If my mother had a friend coming to tea and we sat in with them, we weren't allowed to interrupt, and wouldn't have dreamed of doing so. Now I see parents break off from adult conversation for every tiny niggle and request from their children and you never seem to be able to finish what you were saying.

Children really can be taught to wait until a sentence is finished before they interrupt, and then to say, 'May I ask you something?' Recently I came across a family, on holiday, which had six children, including triplets. The parents were having lunch with us and some other friends outside on the beach and it turned out to be a master class in politeness and manners. While the adults were chatting over lunch, the children would come to the table, stand there quietly and then say sorry to interrupt but, 'Mummy, can I get my float from the car?' or 'Daddy, may I have a drink?' I was impressed, and it was such a pleasure to be able to have our conversation without endless interruptions from the little ones.

I'm sounding off a bit, I know! The thing is, social conventions often go from one extreme to another. I think we had to be too quiet as kids, but I think today's kids interrupt too easily, and sometimes it's all about them. The balance needs to be somewhere in the middle, and perhaps for the next generation of parents, it will be.

The other thing I think many parents do today is drive themselves crazy with an endless schedule for their children. They rush from one class and activity to another, keeping them occupied every hour of the day, which I think is not only exhausting for both parent and child, but is also not particularly good for the child. I think children need a bit of quiet time to themselves, just to think and read and dream and play. It was easier for me when I was a young mum. I used to get together for a cup of tea with my good friend Anne, who lived eight doors away, and whose children were the same ages as mine. We would do our housework in the mornings and then meet in the afternoons at her place or mine, and while we had a cuppa and a chat we would say to the children, 'Go off and play,' and they did.

Of course there's a balance to be found — as

always. I'm not saying that classes and activities outside school hours aren't a good thing. Children need to be encouraged to learn new things, use their talents and abilities and stick with commitments, and extracurricular activities can provide wonderful opportunities for all these things. But children also need free times, and days when they can come home and simply play so they're not totally exhausted by Friday.

One thing I admire a lot is how hands-on and involved today's parents are. I can't confess to turning up at every rugby match my sons played in, but my son Paul works hard all week and then on Saturdays and Sundays he and Sandy are there on the touchline, or at the football or cricket or swimming, supporting Jake and Beau in the sports they love. Parents really do want their children to be confident and to feel good about themselves, and giving them this kind of support goes a long way towards building a child's self-belief.

While many parents are so much more considerate of their children's feelings, and this can only be a good thing, I think sometimes it makes them a bit cautious about insisting on manners. I love it when a child rings to thank me for a gift, or writes me a thankyou note; it makes such a difference and warms the old cockles. It's not the thankyou itself, but that they are taught to appreciate. However, children do need adults to stand over them and teach them that's what you do, until it become automatic. No child says, 'Oh gosh, I must sit down and write my thankyous,' they need to be taught and it stands them in good stead for adulthood.

Most grandparents do learn to zip their lip when it comes to 'in my day' speeches. We don't want to bore the pants off everyone, and we know times, and parenting wisdoms, have changed. But of course the temptation to interfere is always there, especially when you've had years of being in charge of your own household — it's not easy to step back and recognise that the person in charge now is your child, or their partner.

I have tried very hard, over the years, to zip my lip, but there was one occasion when I forgot my own rule and was reminded of it all too clearly! We were all in France on holiday and an argument broke out between my son's children and my daughter's. They were very young then and it was just a squabble, but I leaped in, wanting everything to be calm and cosy. It backfired on me, because the parents got involved and they all looked at me as if to say 'Mind your own business'.

I should have left it to the parents to sort out their children. But of course when you're in your own home it's your prerogative to lay down the basic rules, such as what time meals will be and so on. But you still can't just start disciplining your grandchildren in front of their parents, no matter where you are.

The best way to say something, if you need to, is gently, as a suggestion rather than an imperative. Rather than saying, 'You really ought to put that child to bed,' you can say, 'I wonder if he's tired. How about I take him upstairs and read him a story?' That way it is an offer that can be gratefully accepted, rather than a critical interference.

The thing about advice, generally, is that it's really lovely to be asked, but unless you're asked, don't proffer it. For example, Russ and Caron always used to ask me to come and look at a house they were thinking of buying, and I was pleased as punch to be asked for my opinion. And more recently, when Charlie decided he wanted to go to boarding school for the sixth-form years, Russ phoned and asked me to go and see the school with Charlie, to see whether I felt it was really right for him, and to be sure he really wanted to go. I was delighted to be asked and Charlie and I went down, looked around the school and went for tea afterwards so that we could chat about it. It was a special day for the two of us. I thought the school was fantastic and it was clear that Charlie really wanted to go there. Boarding school at 16 is closer to university than to the grim Victorian boarding schools of the past. So I was able to tell Russ that I thought it was absolutely the right thing to do.

What I and many other grandparents have discovered is that when it comes to advice, less is more. The less you volunteer your opinions, the more you seem to be asked for them, and it feels so much better that way around.

On the other hand, there are rare times when we feel we simply must speak up about something that is important. And finding a way to do this tactfully can be a bit of a minefield.

One grandmother I spoke to told me that she generally tried hard not to interfere with her son and daughter-in-law's parenting, and in most areas she felt they did a very good job, but on one occasion she felt she had to step in. This was when she noticed that her eight-year-old grand-daughter was putting on weight at an alarming rate.

'She was getting very plump,' the grandmother told me. 'I was worried, because apart from the danger to her health my granddaughter told me she was being teased at school. I thought hard about it and decided I needed to say something to my son and his wife. They were feeding their daughter too much of the wrong foods, but how could I tell them that without offending them?

'In the end I said, 'I think you're great parents and you do so much for your child, so I hope you won't mind if I mention something I'm a little worried about. She's putting on quite a bit of weight, so I wonder if perhaps she's slipped into a few unhealthy snacking habits.'

'My son was a bit huffy and said he thought she was fine, but my daughter-in-law said she's been worried too, and we had a very positive discussion about my granddaughter's diet and how it could be gently adjusted.

'I felt very relieved, firstly because the problem was going to be addressed and my granddaugh-ter would be helped, and secondly because I'd managed to get it out in the open without causing too much offence.'

I think most of us can sympathise with this grandmother's feelings. In many cases it's *how* you ask it or the tone in saying it. It's never easy finding a way to tackle a sensitive problem. But being thoughtful and tactful can go a long way. So before you speak out, think about how to include something positive towards the parents in what you say, and how to get the message across without sounding critical or judgemental. If the grandmother in this story had said something like, 'That child's too fat,' or 'You're overfeeding her,' then the conversation might have ended with her son and daughter-in-law telling her not to interfere.

The key to successful interventions is to make very few, and to keep them cheerful, friendly and warm. Young parents need to feel that we believe in them and trust them to get it right for their own children. They want our love and support and backup, not our lists of do's and don'ts. They want us to be there, in the background, being kind and helpful, not taking centre stage or adding to the pressures on them.

One grandmother I know was so opinionated and demanding that her daughter was never able to relax when she was around. I found this sad, because the grandmother didn't realise how difficult she was being, and the daughter didn't want to hurt her mother's feelings by telling her to stop behaving like a spoilt child and start being the granny the family needed. I'm afraid that particular grandmother never did change, and as a result she's not at all close to her grandchildren, because she never learned to take a real interest in them.

That's one of the keys to good grandparenting, I think: taking an interest. A good grandparent wants to know all about their grandchildren. What are their tastes, their hopes and dreams, their best and worst subjects at school? Who are their friends? What do they like doing best? What scares them and what makes them laugh? If you are too critical, you don't have enough time to be curious and to learn.

Here's what some grandparents have said about the giving of advice and discipline in general:

Rose: My views are shrugged off. I'm told things have changed. They either consult a parenting book or ask her best friend who had a baby about a year before her. I don't agree with baby bath products, I think they dry the skin and my granddaughter occasionally has small patches of eczema. I've told my daughter-in-law this is what it is, but it's shrugged off and she continues to use bubble bath — because her friend says it's all right. I no longer give advice, it saves feeling rejected.

Mark: My grandson Jo has the most varied diet I have ever seen for a one-year-old. I'm quite amazed by what he eats, and impressed too. He can pop olives into his mouth like sweeties. How children have changed.

Jackie: Both girls are far more safety conscious than we were and much more influenced by childrearing information from their friends and the internet. They rely on following perceived wisdom more than we did but they also have a wider circle of friends and family who live near them to call on for help. We were very isolated when our own children were small, with substantially older grandparents who were in no position to drop tools and run to help them. Modern economics dictate that all four parents go to work so both babies are in nurseries for the majority of the week. My eldest daughter doesn't see her daughter from Tuesday evening until Thursday evening, which I find quite sad. On the other hand, both fathers are much more involved with their babies than my husband or his peer group were and share parenting responsibilities much more equitably.

Molly: I think the parents should be left to make their own rules. I find it's best not to give too much advice unless asked; just try to keep quiet even though sometimes you're pretty sure you know best! When the children are staying with you, you can make the decisions, but not if the parents are there.

Gayle: I approved of most of our son and daughter-in-law's childrearing methods except for keeping my granddaughter up late when she was obviously exhausted. They have always taken her to parties and what I felt were adult events, regardless of how late they were. However, she doesn't seem to have suffered and is far more confident in adult company that our boys were. So maybe they were right and I was wrong.

Sandra: My opinions on these subjects were usually received happily by my son and his wife

— providing I was subtle in voicing my views. However, my daughter didn't seem to appreciate my 'expert' experience and would remind me that her children were hers and not mine!

Dianne: I don't have the energy for rules and regulations. I only see my grandchildren once a week and I don't want to fight with them or strongly discipline them. I see my role as being their friend and a slightly naughty influence. We have lots of silly conversations about poo-poo. I want us to have a jolly friendship.

I think most grandparents would echo a number of things that have been said here. We want to be liked, and loved by our grandchildren; we don't want to do the heavy disciplining. But at the same time it can be quite hard to stand back and see things being done that are so different to the way you have always done them — particularly if you believe them to be wrong.

The important thing to remember is that pontificating gets you nowhere; what your children want from you is to be a good granny or granddad and be nice. They don't want you interfering in how they bring up their children — they want you to be loving and kind and for their children to adore you and for you to be proud of them, and of their children. And in the end that's what most grandparents want too.

My Grandad

When I go to my grandad's house I love walking his dog. Grandad always has a surprise for me, he is a bit wrinkly, but he is still fantastic.

by Caitlin 10 years

7

The In-laws and the Outlaws

When your son or daughter marries, you become a mother- or father-in-law to their partner. And this can, despite everyone's best efforts, be a tricky role to manage. For mothers-in-law in particular, the path to harmonious family relationships can be a little rocky, at best! Men seem to be a bit calmer and more laid back. It's no coincidence that many comedians have relied on a staple diet of jokes about mothers-in-law (remember Les Dawson?). Here are just a few of the good old stalwarts people have chuckled at for years:

What's the definition of mixed emotions? When you see your new mother-in-law backing off a cliff in your new Mercedes.

My mother-in-law called today. I knew it was her: when she knocked on the front door all the mice threw themselves on the traps!

A woman woke her husband in the middle of the night and told him, 'There's a burglar downstairs in the kitchen and he is eating the cake that my mother made for us.' The husband said, 'Who shall I call, the police or an ambulance?'

131

Getting it right is a tough call, and most of us trip up at times. So why is it sometimes so difficult to be an in-law? Perhaps the roots of the problem lie in a mother or father's closeness to their son or daughter. When your adult or almost-adult child finds a life partner, or marries, it often feels as though you are losing them. Sometimes it's hard to let go and to welcome the new partner no matter who it is, and it's easy to convince yourself that this interloper isn't good enough for your boy or girl. I'm exaggerating, I know — not many mothers or fathers-in-law actually see their offspring's partner as an interloper. But some do, and for the rest of us there's often at the very least a little caution about whether this is the 'right' person, even though your child has grown up and is entitled to make his or her own choices. Those thoughts can go through your head no matter how hard you try to chase them away. Will they look after and love your son or daughter the way you have since birth? Are they really suited to each other? Will it last?

When Caron first started dating boys, I wondered whether I'd ever really feel she'd met the right person. I was lucky, because when Caron met Russ he was so clearly right for her that all my doubts melted away. I always knew he would protect and take care of her, and he always did. Russ loved Caron, and it showed. Not only that, but he was kind and considerate towards all of us in Caron's family. He became like my own son — and when Caron was ill he took care of her and cherished her to the end.

As I've mentioned before, girls go home to their mums, and when Caron was alive I felt I could go into her home at any time, even if she was at work. I could see the boys, read them a story, play with them, go home happy and never see Caron.

When it comes to daughters-in-law, you don't feel as if you have the same right of access, unless you have an extraordinary relationship with your daughter-in-law. Mine, Sandy, is a wonderful mum to Jake and Beau and we see them all the time. But I would never dream of just turning up at the door — I always feel it's more appropriate to make a phone call and say, 'Are you in today? Is it all right to pop by?' I know Sandy has a busy life and it wouldn't feel right to just arrive.

For me being a mother-in-law has, for the most part, been straightforward. I have many friends, men and women, who feel the same way, and get along well with their son- or daughter-in-law. But the bottom line is that it's different to dealing with your own child, and for some it hasn't been at all easy, and relationships are fraught, tense and difficult to manage.

One of the complications, and the reason why it is more often mothers-in-law and daughters-in-law who fall out, is that most mothers are inevitably and naturally closer to their daughters than to their daughters-in-law. This can lead to real differences when it comes to access to grandchildren, and that in turn can lead to conflict.

When Caron's children were small I saw a

great deal of them, simply because Caron and I saw each other several times during the week. There was a natural, easygoing familiarity between us that meant we knew we were welcome in one another's homes, at any time, so I could drop by unannounced and see her and the boys, or even just spend time with them, if Caron was away.

Of course this can't be the same with a daughter-in-law, at least not in most cases. Your daughter-in-law will probably be close to her own mother and family, and will want them around, while as her mother-in-law you have to learn to take a back seat and wait until you are invited to come round, or at the very least phone and ask if you can come by, rather than just turning up.

I have come across a few grandmothers who are extremely close to their daughters-in-law, and who share a real bond. This is more likely when the daughter-in-law's own mother is not around, perhaps because she has died, or lives far away abroad, or for some other reason. In such cases a mother-in-law can become a mother-substitute and both sides can enjoy a deep and fulfilling relationship. But for most of us it's a question of respecting one another's boundaries and treating one another with warmth, friendship and consideration.

There are some cases, though, where relationships between in-laws are thorny from the start. It's not always either the mother-in-law or the daughter-in-law's 'fault' when this happens. There can be a natural wariness, or even a mild jealousy, which can be interpreted as hostility, and things can rapidly deteriorate out of misunderstanding more than anything else. Most of us would prefer to get on with our in-laws and will make an effort to smooth things over, but sometimes our best efforts simply go amiss.

When a grandchild comes along, if relationships within the family have been difficult or stormy, it's a wonderful opportunity to heal things and work towards a much better understanding. If this happens then everyone is better off — especially the new baby, who will benefit hugely from warmer relations between the adults around him or her.

If at all possible, use the birth of a baby as a chance to do things differently; to be warmer, kinder, more helpful and compassionate. When your son or daughter becomes a parent it's an incredibly moving experience. You are flooded with love for the baby, and for your child, who is now responsible for another, tiny, person. This warmth of feeling can be extended to your son- or daughter-in-law. It's just as huge an event for them, so take the opportunity to let go of any negative feelings you've had in the past, and extend goodwill and kindness to them. A hug at this stage can heal a thousand tiny hurts.

Wendy tells a fascinating story of the changing relationship with her daughter-in-law:

'When my son Tom first brought his new girlfriend Lisa to meet us, I liked her. She seemed like a strong character, and I felt that would be good for Tom. She was polite to us and I was impressed that she was working so hard on her studies and was determined to succeed. Tom is a much milder type, he enjoys having fun and isn't very ambitious, so I hoped they would balance one another.

'Tom and Lisa married three years later and it was really after their wedding that things began to change. I felt Lisa became much more possessive towards Tom — he was her territory — and tried to keep me and my husband away. She would make excuses when I invited them over to dinner, and they hardly ever asked us over. I felt excluded from my son's life, and that hurt. I blamed Lisa because I know how easygoing Tom is and that he wouldn't have any reason to push us away — we've always been so close to him.

'On the occasions when we did get together I felt Lisa was very critical. I once took them a bowl I had made in my pottery class and she said, 'It's not really my style,' and walked away. Another time we bought Tom a shirt for his birthday and she said, 'It doesn't suit him,' and we never saw him wear it.

'I puzzled about what was wrong, but I couldn't get to the bottom of it. My husband and I asked ourselves if we had done something to offend her, but we just didn't know. We both felt very sad and hurt and, yes, very angry at times. It was hard to behave warmly towards Lisa when I felt she was keeping me from my only son.

'Then they announced that they were going to have a baby. Naturally we were excited, and hoped to be as involved as possible. But I worried about whether we would get to see much of our grandchild, even though Tom and Lisa only lived a few streets away from us in Newcastle.

'Lisa's mother, who lives in Scotland, came down for the birth, which I understand — after all, girls want their mums around at that time. We waited until we were invited to go and meet our new grandson, Robbie. When we got to the hospital I made sure that the first thing I did was congratulate Lisa, give her a big hug and hand her a baby blanket I had made. She gave me a warm hug back and I could see that something had changed — she had become a mother and there was a softness about her that I hadn't seen before. She realised what being a parent meant.

'From then on things were much better between us. We offered to have Robbie one day a week, to give Lisa and Tom a break, and they accepted, so we were able to really get to know our grandson from the start. When Lisa went back to work we had Robbie for two days a week, and we've done that for the past couple of years.

'What shifted in our relationship with Lisa? I think she began to understand how deeply a mother feels for her child, and how it must be for us, as Tom's parents. And I think loving her own baby made her feel fulfilled, and so less possessive towards Tom. We played our part in healing things too, by coming forward, after the birth, and treating her with real warmth and openness. I remembered what it was like to give birth, how special that is, and just felt it wasn't the time for a grudge, or bitterness.

'We managed to bridge the gulf that was growing between us and our daughter-in-law, and I'm so glad we did, because our grandson means the world to us.

'We've never really talked about what happened, but recently Lisa said something that gave me a clue. We were laughing about something Tom said and she said to me, 'You were such a perfect mum; I thought Tom would always compare me to you.' I was surprised — I had been a far from perfect mother — and touched also, as I realised that Lisa's prickliness was probably self-doubt and a feeling of inadequacy.'

Wendy's story is an encouraging and heart-warming one. It really is worth putting differences aside and trying to heal any breach. However, sadly, there are times when this isn't what happens, and things remain at an impasse. And of course it isn't just with daughters-in-law that relationships can become strained. Recently I met a grandmother who had a very difficult relationship with her son-in-law, which only became worse after her daughter died. I'll let Jill tell her story:

'To be honest my relationship with my son-in-law Mark had always been difficult. Tensions arose more or less six months after I first was introduced to him. Alarm bells began to ring when I witnessed the way he spoke to his mother. He was really rude to her. He also appeared to be incapable of saying a good word about anybody. He was very critical.

'My daughter Georgia and I had always been

very close but I noticed she'd phone me every day after Mark had gone to work to have a chat. Then we'd often meet up and go shopping. Looking back, I think she called after he left as she wanted to spend time with me but not necessarily let Mark know. I never discussed it with her. I didn't want to upset her home life. She loved Mark and he loved her, so I accepted him but he never accepted me.

'I think he has a very jealous nature when it came to sharing Georgia with me.

'When they got married I wanted to contribute but he wanted his family to pay. I insisted and sold my house to do it. Georgia thought I was mad but that's how much she meant to me. I was a single parent and had her with me until she was 29. We'd been through a lot together. I wanted to contribute to her wedding and I wanted to continue to be a big part of her life.

'I suspect our close mother and daughter relationship caused tensions between Georgia and Mark. He always wanted his parents to come on holiday but Georgia was equally strong willed and if she wanted me to come on holiday I was coming.

'One holiday before she fell ill we went out for a meal and Taylor, sitting in his highchair, kept asking to sit on my knee, saying 'Nanny's lap'.

'Mark reacted so aggressively, literally yanking Taylor out of the highchair and pulling him outside. I was horrified and stood up and walked out. When Georgia came to find me I told her, 'I'm sorry but I can't watch that behaviour.'

139

'I don't know if they rowed about it later but in hindsight Mark must have known how I felt about it and probably didn't like it.

'I understand that he was bullied at school and I think perhaps he had an inferiority complex. He always wanted to control situations and didn't like to be undermined. So when Georgia started being sick, with terrible headaches, as her mum I kept nagging her to go to the hospital, which got Mark's back up. It was only when she collapsed that he took her to hospital. To our horror an MRI scan revealed she had a large brain tumour and it was inoperable. We were going to lose her.

'Action was immediately taken to try to prolong her life. There was more radiotherapy and a cocktail of chemotherapy courses. Meanwhile Mark gave up work to look after her, but he also took over her life.

'At first I noticed that Georgia would call me every day at 8.45am and 2.45pm, which must have been the times when Mark was taking Taylor to school and then picking him up again. I suspected she did this to avoid an argument.

'But Georgia got sicker and sicker. Needles were shoved in her left, right and centre and she blew up like a balloon because of the steroids. She was too ill to call me every day and our contact became less frequent. I was desperate to see her, and to help with the boys, but Mark seemed agitated whenever I got in touch, and no matter how hard I tried he always kept me away.

'Rather than ask me to take or pick Taylor up from school he'd ask his own mother, who lived much further away. He and Georgia lived just around the corner from me, but suddenly he was checking her into hotels to be alone with her. I felt pushed out and unwanted.

'When Georgia was at her sickest it became a real struggle to see her. It was like a living nightmare. All I wanted was to care for her. And when my beautiful daughter slipped away, Mark once again took control.

'I wasn't allowed to see her in the chapel of rest until after he and his parents had visited and he decided where her ashes would go.

'Even the headstone excludes me, mentioning Georgia as a beloved wife and mother but nothing about her being my daughter.

'I was devastated without Georgia but at least I still had her boys, Taylor and Nat. I asked to be able to spend time with them in my own home or to take them out for the day but Mark said I could visit once a week and that was it.

'Can you imagine what it's like going to my daughter's house and sitting in her front room and her not being there? And soon there was no sign of Georgia anywhere. Looking around the house you'd think she never existed. All her ornaments and every trace of her had gone — totally heartbreaking.

'From day one I wasn't allowed to spend time alone with Taylor and Nat. When I'm with them Mark sits in a chair or on the computer listening. If I take the children out into the garden he'll come out. He watches me the whole time.

'I once asked him why I wasn't allowed the children by myself and he went purple with rage.

' 'Because you are sick in the head,' he told me. 'I will never forgive you. You didn't leave me and Georgia alone when she was dying.'

'He also told me I was 'the mother from hell' and that all Georgia's problems were down to me. I brought Georgia up on my own and I probably wasn't the best of mothers, but I thought that was utterly unnecessary.

'To begin with Taylor would react very badly when it was time for me to leave. He'd come screaming to the door saying, 'Please, Nanny, I want to come and live with you.'

'I could tell that Mark hated this and it probably made things worse. But it also tore me to pieces. It was so hard for me to have to walk away, knowing I couldn't do anything.

'After six or seven months Taylor stopped asking and now he can sometimes be quite spiteful towards me. More than once Mark has told me to 'get out of his house' and sometimes now Taylor mimics him. I feel like Mark is brainwashing the boys and turning them against me.

'At the end of the day my concern isn't for me. It's for what he's doing to the kids. Nat is three and a half and still in nappies, he can't speak properly and it breaks my heart. I don't interfere, though, as I know that will be the end of my contact with the children.

'In some ways that hour with my grandchildren keeps me alive, but it is also like torture. It should be the most wonderful thing, spending time with my grandsons, but I dread it because of their father. He just sits there listening to

My Grandma is a very nice person and she always lets me have sweets when I see her. She always make's me smile when she talkes. She's a good artist and some time's she shows me things.

By Josh
Aged 8

every single word and I can feel his eyes boring through me. Then he announces that it's time for bed.

'I just remind myself that some grandparents have no contact at all and I should cherish every moment, and I make sure that when I walk in there for my hour I always treat Mark with respect, and I try not to do anything to upset him, otherwise I won't see them at all.

'I do my best for the boys every week and always find them something different and new to interest them. I play with them and make them laugh. Sometimes I take them out into the garden, where they jump all over me and we play football.

'But it is also very painful. I used to have one or both of them almost every day when Georgia was alive and now Taylor has told me that 'Daddy throws the presents away' after I leave.

'My big worry is that by the time my grandchildren are old enough to make their own decisions about me they will have come completely under their father's influence. If only I could have them now and again — just for half a day. They are all I have left of my daughter and I see her in them all the time. I get my one hour a week, yet I know Mark's parents see them every single day.

'I also have to endure six weeks over the summer when I can't see my grandsons, as Mark says they are on holiday. At the start of the year he gave me a calendar with all the weeks highlighted of their holidays when I'm not able to have them.

'When I can't see the boys, it is my good friend Rachel that I turn to. She lives in Spain and invites me to go out to see her. She's absolutely marvellous. She gives me loads of things to do and gets me working all the time. I'm better over there.

'I've been seeing a counsellor, and she has warned me that one day soon Mark may stop all contact, so for now I do my best to put on a brave face, go round and make the most of my precious time with my grandsons.

'Recently I have been making them memory books. I'm going to include pictures of their mum growing up and tell them all about her. I also have some nice messages from them stored on my Ansaphone. They are giggling and sound excited to be leaving me a message. It's the little things like that which help me to cope. I just pray that the boys will always know how much I love them.'

Jill's story is terribly sad. As a mother who has also lost my daughter I feel deeply for her, and I know how vital and healing it is to spend time with your grandchildren. I hope things will improve for Jill. She is making the most of the time she does have with her grandsons, and that's the right thing to do.

Sometimes, even when things have been tricky between in-laws, there is light at the end of the tunnel. Another story I heard recently was from Celeste, who has been through many struggles with her daughter-in-law. Celeste is French, her daughter-in-law English, which hasn't helped either of them to understand the other. There is always the cultural difference. Celeste is also a strong-minded and determined person, who always says it like she sees it. In a friend this is an endearing quality, but in a mother-in-law it can be interpreted as bossiness, or poking your nose in.

Here is Celeste's account of her relationship with her daughter-in-law:

'I have two children, a son and a daughter, but only my son has children. He and my daughter-in-law have three children, aged ten, five and two. It's fantastic having grandchildren, I'm so in love with them. We see our children in our grandchildren and it takes us back to those magical days when they were small.

'In France grandparents are very important; in most families the grandparents are close and are very involved. I know it's been difficult for my daughter-in-law to understand the closeness we have in France because in her family it wasn't like that. My son doesn't understand it either, because sadly he didn't ever know his grandparents — they died before he was born.

'When my daughter-in-law was pregnant I would go to visit with a big dish of food, wanting to help out, and she would take it with a look as if to say, 'Huh, she's saying I can't cook.' My daughter would have said, 'Bring more!' My daughter-in-law saw it as an attack.

'My son and daughter-in-law live near us in France, and I have always insisted on seeing my granddaughters at least once a week, but I've had to fight my corner. Both my son and his wife are very possessive and controlling. I see my grandchildren every Friday, and every Thursday night I have to phone to confirm. I would never dream of going to my daughter-in-law's home without phoning. Nothing is automatic, and nor can I take anything for granted.

'When I collect the children from school they run into my arms shouting, 'Grandma! Grandma!' Then I take them to our house on the beach — we are very lucky to live there — and they can run free and enjoy all the seaside things. When they stay the night, which they do in the holidays, we go out with torches at night and have a midnight feast, with sweets and crisps and all kinds of treats, and they absolutely love it.

'Being a Latin grandmother I would bring clothes for the children, but my daughter-in-law didn't like that, because she hadn't chosen them, so I had to stop. I've learned not to take food, or clothes, so now I stick to toys and little gifts for the children.

'I think my daughter-in-law felt threatened by me, and I think my son does anything for peace. He adores his wife and if she wants something he will try to do it.

'I said to my son, 'The love I have for my grandchildren is so different to the love you and your wife have for them. There's no comparison. They need both.'

'If she was my daughter I would speak out. I could say, 'Oh come on, that's ridiculous,' when she's unreasonable. But with a daughter-in-law you can't do that. I have had to learn to hold back, to be reserved. It isn't always easy — I am a strong character.

'And so many girls are hostile to their mothers-in-law. One girl told me she wouldn't let her mother-in-law see her child until he was two, because she 'wouldn't be the right influence'. Another told me her mother-in-law was 'nuts' and that she wouldn't let her daughter stay in her house overnight. It's so unfair. I am a mother-in-law and I know how much you suffer when you are cut out. We have an unfair image, and that's sad.

'At one time I was so distressed about my relationship with my daughter-in-law that I went to a psychologist. He said to me, 'You're quite an adamant person. You say, 'We're going to the beach today.' You've got so used to being in charge. What if you say, 'Would it be a good idea to go to the beach?' Simply put the suggestion into the mix and see what other people say. Then if you go to the beach it is everybody's decision, they all feel consulted.'

'This was useful for me. I suppose, like many mothers, I was used to making the decisions. Since I have stuck only to suggestions, things are going better. I think my daughter-in-law is slowly beginning to understand that it's good for children to have loving grandparents. She knows, I hope, that she and my son are number one in their children's lives, but it's important that they know their grandparents.'

I think Celeste put her finger on something when she said that perhaps her daughter-in-law felt threatened by her. And in Wendy's story it sounds as though there might be a similar scenario. Perhaps, because a boy has grown up

148

loving his mother, subsequently girlfriends and wives can feel unsure of themselves. And perhaps mothers, even when they're well-intentioned, can find it a little hard to let go.

So what do other grandparents think of their sons- or daughters-in-law?

Jackie: We adore our two sons-in-law and, as parents of girls, we are delighted to have additions to our family who are just the sort of young men we would have wished for in any sons of our own. We don't intrude into their relationships with our daughters. That is a contract whose terms can only be determined by them. If anything, we are possibly more likely to sympathise with our sons-in-law over issues as we are well acquainted with the whims of our daughters! At least one of them has married her father and if she doesn't know how to handle his idiosyncrasies after watching her mother do so for 30 years then she never will.

Molly: We're very lucky as all our children's partners are wonderful, so it's been like gaining additional sons and daughters. However, they all have very strong characters and getting everyone to agree on family holidays, etc., can be horrendous. Luckily our children and their partners are all as bad as each other.

Gayle: I was asked to be around during the period of my daughter-in-law's stay in hospital, but once she came home it was made plain I should go home. I was a little disappointed, but

I do remember feeling a little crowded by my in-laws when I wanted time to adjust to motherhood and lack of sleep, so I understood. My son was very protective of his wife, and that impressed me as I didn't have the same respect from my husband.

Sandra: My relationship with my son's partner was one of gratitude and possibly seeing her as the one to make my son more responsible and grown up. Though in time I did begin to worry, as her aspirations seemed to be over and above their means, and I foresaw (correctly as it turned out) this might lead to financial pressures for them. I had no issues with my future son-in-law to begin with — until I realised he was not a particularly practical person. Neither was our daughter, and I worried about how they could possibly cope with those issues — but it actually turned out to have the rewarding result of turning my daughter into a truly hands-on person in her own right, thus giving her confidence that she had badly lacked before — so, happy ending!

Sadie: I have had huge difficulties with my son's wife. She is self-centred, bad-mannered, disrespectful and domineering. She has stormed out of my house or away from my dining table on numerous occasions, and on others she merely decides not to turn up when invited. They decided to go to Italy and marry secretly but did not invite any parents or friends. I found this deeply hurtful as I have always had an open, friendly, caring relationship with my son. Being excluded from his wedding was really the beginning of an ongoing series of disappointments. The relationship between my daughter-in-law and my ex-husband, with whom I am very friendly, has completely broken down through her ill manners and her obstinate determination not to allow any member of her family to visit him in Africa, despite the fact that I was brought up there, and her husband, my son, was born there. My ex-husband has offered more than once to pay for them all to fly out and stay with him.

So, a very mixed set of responses, which only goes to show that in every family the situation is different and in every relationship, good and bad, there are two sides. Here I have only looked at the perspective of the grandmother, in her role as a mother-in-law. I'm sure the sons- and daughters-in-law might see things very differently. But that's the point — people are so very different, and it is only with tolerance, acceptance and generous hearts that we can bridge what sometimes seems like a huge gulf, and find common ground.

Grannys hair is white
as snow, shes a bit plump —
and that doesnt matter!

When granny comes to
my house, I can hear her
stick going clinck, clinck, clinck-
Then her lovely, warm voice
calls "anybody home!"

fiona
aged 10

Clink
Clink
Clink

8

Having Fun

The great blessing of being a grandparent is that we are allowed to have fun with our grand-children — and lots of it. We get to do the silly things, the giggly things, the enlightening, entertaining and daft things. While parents have to discipline and, for the most part be sensible, grandparents — although responsible — can be co-conspirators and instigators of good times.

What grandparents so often have that parents don't have is time. And there is no greater gift for a grandchild than *time*.

We all despair, on occasions, about what presents to give our grandchildren. Ask them what they want for Christmas or their birthday and many of today's children will say 'I dunno' because they already have so many toys, games, DVDs, bicycles, skateboards, gadgets and gizmos that they honestly can't think of anything else to ask for. I always feel a bit frustrated when that happens because in my day — now I promised I wasn't going to use that expression — but way back when I was little we always had things we dreamed of and longed for. I remember wondering whether I would ever be lucky enough to have that doll in the shop window, or a new bike instead of a secondhand one, or a doll's house. I think aspiration is a good thing,

153

and it's a shame when children have nothing to dream of, work towards and earn.

Joan Collins, herself a grandmother to three gorgeous grandchildren, wrote about this in a recent article. Commenting on today's mini-me generation of have-it-all children, she says, 'When I was a girl I was lucky if my parents even acknowledged my existence, let alone followed me around eager to please me.

'I was lucky to get one present at Christmas and the same for my birthday, when the entertainment usually consisted of having a couple of school friends over for tea, a cucumber sandwich and a piece of cake.

'Hundreds and sometimes thousands of pounds are spent on children's parties and presents now, and Christmas is all about what you can get, instead of what it means to give.'

I can't help agreeing with Joan. However, that's simply the way it is today. And it is also a reminder that what grandparents really can give that will always be valuable is time and attention.

Don't be fooled into thinking that your grandchildren are too busy or too involved with their friends to want time with you. If you genuinely want to be with them, finding out about their lives and enjoying their company, then they will respond with interest and delight. And if you can find something to do together that you both enjoy, it can lead to many happy hours in one another's company.

As children get that bit older, their lives get more and more busy and grandparents have to learn how to tap into their timetable within the school term, when downtime is limited. One of the things I love to do is take my grandsons out to tea. I sometimes go over to Hampton Court, where both Paul, my son, and Russ, my former son-in-law, live with their families, and take all four of my grandsons out for their favourite pizza (it always seems to be pizza!). That way I get to catch up on their news and lives while we enjoy lots of goodies and, of course, our family favourite: tea.

Once they get into their teens, you have to move with the times. It's no longer enough to take them to the local park; you've got to think about what will interest them. I sometimes take them tenpin bowling, because that's something I can do with them. I'm not much good at kicking a football, but I can hold my own in a bowling alley and sometimes, to their surprise, I'll even win.

As they grow towards their later teens I do try to be a bit of a 'cool' granny by organising treats like tickets to rock and pop concerts, or trips to places they've never been. This is my favourite thing to do, almost my mission, because everybody remembers their 'first times' and I want to give my grandsons that kind of memory.

A couple of years ago Stephen and I took Charlie and Gabriel to New York and we had a marvellous time. My younger son Michael happened to be working there and the boys loved that, because they adore him — he's the cool, with-it uncle. We said to them, 'We're here for you to have fun, so tell us what you want to do and see, and if we can, we'll do it.' We took the ferry to see the Statue of Liberty, we went up the Empire State Building, took them to witness Ground Zero and of course we also wanted to see a Broadway show. The consensus was *Hair*. I hadn't seen it for years and years and I'd forgotten how much nudity there is on stage at times. At one point there were quite a few willies on show and Charlie leaned over to me and said, 'Nana, this is a very racy show for you to take your grandchildren to see!' He was right, but we had a great time and hopefully they'll remember it and laugh for years to come about the time Nana took them to see *Hair*.

More recently, Stephen and I took Jake and Beau to Barbados for the first time. I didn't fancy spending one of my big birthdays at home, so I organised a villa holiday and it turned out a triumph for all of us. Jake and Beau were happy, literally, as sandboys on the beach, while we lapped up the sun, wine and food. The best part, for me, was knowing that as I said goodnight to the boys each evening I would see them again at breakfast in the morning. And hopefully Jake and Beau will always remember their first time on the island of Barbados. They enjoyed it so much they want to make it an annual Easter event.

When my children were small I tried to do something semi-cultural every week. I wanted to show them the world and open their eyes to new experiences. I took them to plays, concerts, opera, ballet, art galleries, museums and every interesting exhibition or event I could find. They didn't always enjoy it, but that wasn't the point, I just wanted to expose them to it and let them take it in and then choose for themselves.

To a lesser extent, and although we certainly haven't gone every week, I've tried to carry that idea on with my grandchildren. And I think this is where grandparents can come into their own. We can take them to things they might never otherwise see — and give their parents a break into the bargain.

There are so many things you can do for free, or for very little cost. In fact nowadays there is more to do and see for free than ever before. Wander down London's South Bank and you'll see a true example of adventurous skateboarding, or even an area of authorised graffiti. Or there's Covent Garden, where you'll find street artists of every kind enchanting crowds of people, especially children. There are jugglers, fire-eaters, human statues, artists and musicians. Then there's the Tate Modern, a wonderful art gallery which is completely free, right next to Shakespeare's Globe, a theatre where you can get the cheapest tickets for very little and watch Shakespeare's plays performed in the open-topped model of his original theatre.

Our older boys love the markets like Camden and Spitalfields on a Sunday morning. They're very fashion-conscious and it's interesting to see how their tastes differ. Gabriel, for example, loves designer labels, while Charlie is into retro. Just like his mum used to do, he prefers shopping in a specialist retro shop or a charity shop. He gets much more excited about bargains such as a leather bomber jacket for £10 than a new designer jacket for £80.

Jake, although he's a bit quieter about his fashion tastes, is still very clear-cut about what he likes. There are times when I've pounded up and down the High Street for so long that I could tell you the entire stocklist of Top Man, River Island, Banana Republic and several other stores.

All over London — and every city and town in Britain is the same — there are fascinating things to do for free, and many more for very reasonable prices. Taking your grandchildren on the bus or train (most children adore public transport) for a day out, with a backpack of sandwiches and a flask of tea (of course), you can have a really special time, and create memories that the children will cherish as they grow older.

If you live in the country there's a whole world of things to do which grandchildren will love. Country grandparents tend to love going out for walks, but in my experience grandchildren often groan if you suggest, 'How about we go out for a nice walk?' Instead, it can work to suggest, 'How about we go hunting / picking berries / wildlife spotting / exploring the jungle?'

A friend of mine used to take her grand-children to the woods and then quietly slip a few little chocolate eggs into the holes in gnarled old tree trunks and then get the children to hunt for them. For years the children believed the eggs were left by the 'chocolate squirrels' and they used to shout, 'Let's go to the Chocolate Woods, Granny,' when they came to stay. It got them out of the house for hours of happy hunting.

Collecting things you find is another wonderful way to fill a 'walk'. Take a bag, or big pockets, and collect conkers, seedpods, pebbles, shells — if you're on the beach — pretty flowers and leaves or anything else you find. If it's berry time you can fill a tub with blackberries and then go home and make a crumble together. Children absolutely love to cook something delicious and then eat it, and creating a flour- and sugar-strewn, warm and cosy kitchen scene is great fun for both adults and children.

Another lovely thing to do — country or town — is put up a tent in the garden and let your grandchildren 'camp' in it for the day. You can take them snacks and treats and put a few cushions and blankets in the tent — it's different and it makes them feel so special and excited. Of course there's plenty to do if you just want to stay at home too. Days out, though very worthwhile, can be pretty tiring, and sometimes it's lovely to curl up, watch a movie with them or choose a book and read to them, play games (Ludo and Scrabble are two of our favourites) or simply chat to them. Most children love to talk and will, with a little gentle prompting and a patient, willing ear, happily tell you about their friends, their pets, their interests and their dreams.

Pets can be a source of enormous fun. A few months after Caron died Charlie turned eleven and Stephen and I wanted to give him a special present. We suggested a puppy, but Russ said that would be a lot of hard work, which we quite understood because at the time he had a huge amount to cope with. We considered getting a tortoise, but they are so expensive; they need special heated glass tanks and they're not really a lot of fun to play with, so we eventually settled on rabbits. Russ and the boys were living in Cornwall at the time, so Stephen and I headed down there with two beautiful black rabbits, a hutch, a big bag of rabbit food and — this made us laugh — two lovely red leads that the boys could use to lead the rabbits around the garden.

Charlie and Gabriel were thrilled and spent many happy hours with their rabbits. They used to play with them, pet them, lead them around and even trained them to sit on their chests while they were watching TV.

They loved them so much that Stephen and I decided to get some rabbits to keep in Sevenoaks, for when all our grandchildren came to visit. We felt that a mutual interest like that would be great in helping to keep the communication lines between older and younger generations open. We went and bought two white rabbits, and installed them in a hutch in our garden. We called them Snowy and Thumper and the children would race out to see them whenever they arrived. We had a lot of fun with them, but unfortunately both sets of rabbits got very busy producing more little rabbits, so that Charlie and Gabriel ended up with eight and Stephen and I ended up with twelve!

When Charlie and Gabriel moved back to London with their dad, a year or so later, it was impractical to take the rabbits with them, so new homes had to be found. We kept ours for a long time after that, but in the end poor Stephen

Naomi Age: 11

My Grandpa is always inventing bits and pieces out of cardboard with his sharp scissors and protective gloves.

Suprise!

I always have a warm welcome and a great suprise from my Grandma.

seemed to be spending most of his time cleaning out the hutches and the boys were beginning to lose interest, so they too were found new homes. But for the time we had them it gave us a fantastic mutual interest with the boys, and something to enjoy together and talk about. These days it's Gemma our King Charles Cavalier who is the 'star'. The boys make such a fuss of her when they see her and they insist she goes everywhere with us.

The thing I like best is to chat and laugh with the boys, when we're all together, and sometimes we like to play 'what if' games. On one occasion we took Charlie and Gabriel out for a meal and they each brought a friend with them. While we were waiting for our meal to come we said, 'What would you do if you won the lottery?'

Jack, Charlie's friend, answered first. 'I'd pay off my mum's mortgage and then save some to buy a house,' he said, solemnly. 'I wouldn't waste any of it.'

Paddy, his brother, said he would help his mummy out, buy a new car for her, give some to charity and buy some nice toys.

When it was Charlie's turn he said he would buy his dad anything he needed, save for a flat, give some to charity and save the rest.

Finally it was Gabriel's go. He didn't hesitate. 'I'd buy a Ferrari, in red or yellow,' he grinned.

'Wouldn't you give any of the money away?' we asked. 'What about the poor children who are hungry?'

Gabriel's face was solemn. 'Name me two,' he said.

I did my best to keep a straight face. 'Seriously, Gabriel, what about all the people who are hungry or don't have homes?'

He paused, and then said, 'Oh, don't worry, I'll send them a few meat pies now and again.'

Times like this have given us a great deal of laughter and joy. You can never predict what children will say or do, they're a source of endless surprises, and that's part of the pleasure of them.

When Caron was ill, she and Russ went to live in Australia for two years, so that she could follow up and research sources of healing. She had discovered an area on the Gold Coast, south of Brisbane, called Byron Bay. It was like a sweet shop for complementary treatments, and the attitude in that area was that it was enough to just 'be'. You didn't have to be anything or anybody, and it seemed to be what Caron needed at that time. She loved the constant sunshine and the feelgood factor there.

It was incredibly hard having the whole family move so far away — after all, no Irish mother wants her children further away than round the corner, but especially when Caron was ill with cancer, that made it almost unbearable. Stephen and I missed them terribly and we went out to visit eight times during that period, often staying for several weeks. It meant putting our working lives on hold, and we were lucky enough to be able to do that, but it was so worth it. As well as worrying constantly about my daughter and wanting to see her and find out how she was, I missed my grandsons and didn't want to lose out on a whole chunk of their lives.

Whenever we arrived in Australia the boys would come racing towards us with shouts of 'Nana' and 'Stevie'. Those hugs and cuddles meant the world to us. And of course they always wanted to know what pressies were in our overstuffed suitcases! Despite Caron battling with cancer, we had some very special times in Australia, because our normally busy lives were on hold. Stephen and I were able to spend a lot of time with the boys, not only picking them up from school, cooking, bathing them and putting them to bed, but having fun all the time with them. Although their mother was ill, and this weighed heavily on all of us, we were in a beautiful place, by the beach, and there was still a great deal of optimism and belief that Caron would recover. She managed her illness magnificently and was always positive in her attitude. The reality is that being around children lightens any scenario; they need to run and play and laugh as much as they need to breathe. And that was good for the rest of us. It kept us positive in our attitude.

We used to spend hours on the beach, running races, building sandcastles, collecting shells and watching the boys learn to surf and splash around in the waves. There was a sense of space and freedom there that was intoxicating. We loved to be outdoors, on the beach, or animal spotting, walking for miles and playing all kinds of outdoor games. The sheer scope of the space in Australia gave us a whole new dimension and the boys were able to run free in a way they perhaps never could have done back home. Life seemed to be lived in T-shirts, shorts and bare feet. Despite everything, it was a happy time, and every photograph of those days was of the family laughing, singing and dancing.

There are a thousand different ways of having fun with your grandchildren. It may mean baking cakes together, watching them dress up and put on little 'shows', reading them stories, going to the park, painting, drawing or just sitting on the grass making daisy chains. What children love most is when you do things with them. So if you feel up to it, run around in the park with them, join them on your stomach in the grass looking at worms, play a leisurely game of rounders or 'it' and sit together on the grass with a simple 'picnic'.

One grandfather I spoke to, David, has three grandchildren, aged nine, five and three.

'We see them every two or three weeks,' he says. 'They stay with us for two or three days and we look forward to it very much. I think grandparents get the fun side of children, because we haven't got all the school issues and the discipline problems.

'My wife feeds them and puts them to bed, but my role is to play with them. I take them to the park and push my granddaughter on the swings, or lift her up to the climbing bars, then I have a little game of football with the boys. I love the park, and I love taking them swimming. We do a lot of reading with them, and colouring, so that they learn about colours and shapes.

'I always think the best part of their visit is at

the beginning and the end of the day. Seeing them come running through the door when they arrive, with all the hugs and hellos, is lovely. Then putting them to bed at night and reading to them. They always say, 'Can we have another story, Granddad?' That always makes me laugh.'

Of course no two grandchildren are alike, and what appeals to one may not appeal to another. But almost every child loves a story, whether you read to them or just make it up as you go along.

Here are some of the things other grand-parents do with their grandchildren:

Mark: We play ball games, blow up balloons and fly them, enjoy 'messy play' with paint, water, play-doh and so on. Pretend vacuuming the floor keeps my grandson occupied for a long period too (although not switched on!), and he has a wooden car to push.

Jackie: We have a large garden and, as both grandchildren live in London, they love the freedom of being outside in the country. We walk and cycle and just take the children with us. I find the internet wonderful for finding toys, clothes and useful gadgets for babies. I love daisy-roots.com for shoes, lulasapphire.com and grannytakesagrip.com.

Molly: Cooking is always good, and chocolate rice krispy cakes are top of our list. Our grandchildren love hide and seek, snap, building bricks, and visits to the zoo and the garden centre, where they can spend hours looking at the plants. All the children know about modern technology so you just have to join them and learn. You can always ask them to show you.

Penny: I play on the Wii, we go to the garden centre to look at the wildlife and I get a coffee! And they love cooking and art — they really enjoy being creative.

Gayle: Our granddaughter lives in the London suburbs, so life here, outside London, is very different. We swim, cook and go out with other neighbouring children. I usually plan an expedition to a hands-on type of venue — a working farm or country park or visiting somewhere of interest and relevant to her school curriculum.

Sandra: I have embraced modern technology! I've had to, because my grandchildren seem to be way ahead all the time and spend their time on computers, Nintendos, etc., leaving little or no time to get outside and *play*! Although their parents do try to make them go out as much as is possible, suggesting healthy outdoor activities and things of interest around them. It's usually me the grandmother unable to keep up!

Roger: I have an iPhone and have downloaded applications for my granddaughter. I doubt my daughter would approve but the little one enjoys it and she learns how to use technology while having fun. She's a bit hamfisted with it at the moment but she is only four. She enjoys putting Humpty back together again and similar things but I like to go beyond nursery stuff and I'm teaching her to recognise birds by sight and sound. I think if things like that are taught at an early age it will become second nature to her. Today she recognised the call of a crow outside after just one session with this application. I only wish I'd had one when my kids were young.

Sadie: I have embraced modern technology but as a grandparent I don't think I need to use it. My eldest grandchild is perfectly happy amusing himself when he stays with me either in the garden or on walks with my dog when we often play 'pooh sticks' in the stream. As I was brought up in the bush in Africa I do not believe children need constant amusement provided by adults. They have such wonderful imagination and are often happiest making up their own games. He joins me visiting my friends and generally does what I do — he seems happy with that! When they are older I hope to take them to visit art museums and National Trust properties.

What a wonderfully wide range of activities these grandparents describe — and I'm sure every grandparent who reads this could add another one or two. Whether it's as simple as giving a toddler a saucepan and a wooden spoon, or some pebbles to put in and out again, or as sophisticated as helping an older grandchild design a website, or taking them to a concert, there are a thousand ways of enjoying time together. And this special time together is a wonderful way of getting to know one another.

A friend of mine was trying to teach his little grandson some maths recently and the two of them were getting a bit fraught with one another. The grandfather was saying, 'No, you've got to do it this way,,' and the grandson's lip was wobbling. Then the little boy's dad stepped in and said to his father, 'Dad, would you stop being heavy and just be a nice granddad?'

It made his father think and after that the maths book was put to one side and the two of them — grandfather and grandson — played card games.

It's worth remembering, too, that sometimes it's the children who make us laugh and show us how to have fun — all we have to do is let them lead the way. So asking, 'What would you like to do?' and then doing it with them for an hour or two is a great way to get close and let them feel they really matter and that you're genuinely interested in them. You've got to be prepared to do whatever they choose, though, whether that's hunting for bugs in the garden, making fudge or checking out a new website.

Whatever you do, have a laugh with your grandchildren. I've heard hundreds of wonderful stories about grandchildren making grandparents laugh (and when you laugh, you can't help but have fun). Here are two of my favourites:

One grandmother I spoke to told me, 'Recently I took my eldest grandson, who is six, to Cornwall. On the way back, after a very happy week together, I was driving on a very busy motorway dotted with numerous cones. It was snowing and visibility was poor so I told him that

I had to really concentrate in such conditions.

''It's God's fault,' he said.

''In that case,' I replied, 'we had better say a prayer.'

''How do we do that?' he said.

''Dear Father God, please let us drive safely through the snow and the traffic so that we get home in one piece,' I said.

'He repeated the prayer and then, after a long silence, he said, 'What colour dress does God wear?'

'It was funny and he made me laugh and I was no longer anxious.'

Another wonderfully funny and touching story came from the American grandparent whose grandchild wrote the following passage in a school essay:

'We always used to spend the holidays with Grandma and Grandpa. They used to live in a big brick house but Grandpa got retarded and they moved to Arizona. Now they live in a tin box and have rocks painted green to look like grass. They ride around on their bicycles and wear name tags because they don't know who they are any more. They go to a building called a wreck centre, but they must have got it fixed because it's all OK now. They do exercises there, but they don't do them very well. There is a swimming pool too, but they all jump up and down in it with hats on.

'At their gate there is a doll's house with a little old man sitting in it. He watches so nobody can escape. Sometimes they sneak out and go cruising in their golf carts. Nobody there cooks, they just eat out. And they eat the same thing every night — early birds. Some of the people can't get past the man in the doll house. The ones who do get out bring food back to the wrecked centre for pot luck. My Grandma says that Grandpa worked all his life to earn his retardment and I should work hard so I can be retarded some day too. When I earn my retardment, I want to be the man in the doll house. Then I will let people out, so they can visit their grandchildren.'

What a reminder of how utterly unique a child's view of life is, and how important it is to let them tell us how they see it, and lead the way for us. No-one knows better than a child how to have fun. They know all about clowning around, horse-playing, joking and teasing. So whatever you do when you are with your grandchildren, enjoy yourselves. The time you have with them passes so quickly, and before you know it they will be grown up. So forget the chores, forget 'sensible' and just have a good time.

I used to live in America but now I live here, so I miss her very much. She is very funny and is always taking us to the park. She is 81 and takes care of her mum, who is 100. It's unbelievable!

By Katie Whitworth aged 8

9

Grandparents and the Law

I think you've got the message by now that I feel incredibly fortunate in being able to see and talk to my grandchildren all the time. I look forward to my time spent with them enormously and if I don't have a date in the diary to see them next then I feel uneasy.

And although I'm a bit of a technophobe, the beauty of modern technology is that once they're of a certain age it always seems possible to keep in touch by phone or text, and sometimes that little message to say 'hi' is all I need for my 'Nana fix'.

Research shows that, thankfully, the majority of grandparents, like me, have regular contact with their grandchildren. A recent survey found that 61 per cent of grandparents see their grandchildren at least once a week, and another 17 per cent see them at least once a month. And grandfathers see their grandchildren just as often as grandmothers — there is no difference between them when it comes to contact.

Most grandparents say they are happy with the contact they have, but for one very significant group of grandparents it is a *very* different story. These are the grandparents who are unable, for various reasons, to see or even have contact with their grandchildren.

I have covered a lot of subjects in my years as a broadcaster, but until recently I didn't know just how hard it is for a grandparent to gain access to their grandchildren if a parent, or stepparent, refuses it. Heartbreakingly, it is estimated that a million grandchildren are denied contact with their grandparents as a result of adoption, divorce, separation or family feuds. Grandparents, quite simply, have no 'rights' in Britain. It's important to point out that we're not talking here about the right to bring them up, or even to influence their lives, but simply the 'right' to see them.

It was only when the Grandparents' Association invited me to attend a reception at 10 Downing Street, hosted by Sarah Brown, wife of the then Prime Minister, that I realised and learned about the full extent of this shocking state of affairs. The aim of the reception was to highlight the plight of those grandparents who have lost access to their grandchildren and to campaign for a change in the law so that grandparents have more right of access. In my naivety I simply assumed that if you had grandchildren who were blood relatives, then it was your right at least to see them.

At the moment the process of applying to the courts is long, complex and expensive, and more often than not ends in disappointment for grandparents.

Some of the stories we heard at that Downing Street reception were tragic. At a time of death or divorce, when a family is already under great strain and children have to cope and adapt, the loss of contact with loving grandparents is a terrible blow. It can become a double loss for children who lose a parent and then grandparents too, and of course it's a double loss for the grandparents as well. Just at a time when children need security and stability, their worlds are turned upside down.

When Caron died in 2004, Charlie was ten and Gabriel was seven and the children and Russ stayed with us in Sevenoaks for almost three months. It seemed the most natural place for them to be. After all, there was an infrastructure; it was like a second home to the children, who had been coming to the house since they were born. Many of their things were there, so it gave them a deep sense of familiarity.

Now spring forward to the time when circumstances had changed and Russ remarried, when the dynamics and practicalities also changed.

Thankfully Russ and Sally always made sure I was still very much part of the children's lives and still do but, inevitably, with a new home setup of their own, I now feel more of an in-law situation where I simply can't just drop in unannounced. And therefore naturally arrangements have to be made to suit everybody, and be put in the diary.

In addition, as they get older the children have developed a life of their own and are involved in so many arrangements: sport, after-school activities, school plays, hanging about with mates in coffee bars and so on — all of which, of course, would have happened in just the same way had Caron still been alive. So inevitably it becomes even harder to find the space for get-togethers and we grandparents have to be prepared to be flexible with our own schedules, to fit in.

These unavoidable shifts in the way things develop have given me a tiny, tiny glimpse into how it might be for those grandparents who lose contact with their grandchildren. After that Downing Street reception I felt very strongly that I wanted to do all I could to highlight the awful loss some grandparents — and their grandchildren — suffer. So I would like to tell some of the stories grandparents have told me, in the hope that we might all pause for a moment and then add our voices to those demanding change.

Clive's story

A few years ago our son Dominic separated from his partner Allie. Right from the beginning Allie was difficult about letting their little boy, Max, who was five, see his dad, or us.

Max used to come on holiday with us, and a couple of months after the breakup we planned to take him away as usual, but when we went to pick him up Allie opened the door, said, 'He's not going,' and slammed the door in my wife's face.

After that arrangements, when there were any, were entirely at Allie's convenience. Sometimes she would refuse to let us see Max, and at other times she used us as last-minute childcare. We never said no, because it was our chance to be with him.

I used to pick Max up from school on a Friday and take him back to his mum on a Saturday morning, but sometimes she'd just call and cancel. Then she would call us asking us to babysit because she wanted to go out. Once she left him with us for a whole weekend without letting us know where she was, or what was happening.

I used to take him to church every Sunday morning, then one day she said, 'Stop taking him to church. It's a bad influence on him.'

Later that year Max broke his leg in two places and he was in Leeds Infirmary for five weeks.

When I went to see him on the first day, his mother said, 'Here's your bloody granddad.'

That was when the real problems started. He asked for me a lot and it made her jealous.

She didn't tell us he'd come out of hospital, so when we rang the hospital to see how he was they said he had gone home.

I went over to see them and took Max a present and at that point Allie's new boyfriend got me by the scruff of the neck and frogmarched me out, telling me not to come back.

Later Allie told my wife Max could come and stay with us in a fortnight but it was soon clear she had no intention of letting him come, and our attempts to arrange to see him were thwarted every time.

We sought advice and went for mediation, and then it went to court.

The first time Allie didn't turn up. The second time it was agreed in court that we'd all get together and talk round a table.

We were offered help by CAFCASS (Children and Family Court Advisory and Support Service) and it was agreed that Max's mum would take him to the CAFCASS office in town on a Saturday morning, so that my son could see him there, but from the start it didn't happen. At first Allie kept claiming that Max didn't want to come, then she just stopped turning up, even though there was a court order saying she had to do it.

Now she's got married to her boyfriend and is distancing Max from us even more.

Last year my wife rang to talk to Max on the phone and asked, 'How come you didn't send your daddy a Father's Day card?'

Max replied: 'Mummy says that Ryan's my dad now.'

These days when my wife rings her up to see how Max is getting on she claims he doesn't want to talk to us. She's influencing him. I call it brainwashing.

Last year, we found out third-hand that Max had a fall at school and broke his wrist. His mother hadn't even bothered to let his dad know.

We managed to get an 'indirect contact' court order that says he's got to write to his dad at least once a fortnight, but it doesn't say anything about the content. Well, some of the letters that come . . . my grandson says things like, 'You've never done anything for me, and you're not interested in me.' It's all lies. When you read the letter you can tell that it's Allie's words.

Max is now nine and it's all going back to court. It's cost me £5,000 so far and it's made me and my wife poorly with stress and anxiety. Grandparents really have no rights, and it's very sad.

Tragically, there are families up and down the country who have a similar story to tell. Separation and divorce is the biggest single cause of grandparents losing touch with their grandchildren. However, while divorce is the primary cause, it's certainly not the only one. In Margaret's case, it was her son who stopped his little boy from seeing his grandmother.

Margaret's story

I don't see my grandchild. I've not seen him since he was six weeks old and he's just over three now. The problem is that my son is very troubled; he has a big drink problem, he has self-harmed a lot and has tried to commit suicide several times.

It all came to a head when he tried to kill himself at my home. I was out doing voluntary work and he let himself in and took 120 of my tablets with three litres of cider.

I came back to find an ambulance outside my house. They had to revive my son twice, but he pulled through. But when I went to see him in hospital I felt certain that he was going to try to kill himself again. I warned the nurses that he might try to do something and he did, he took the light bulb out and slashed his wrists.

When he came out of hospital he stayed overnight with me, but he got into a terrible state and smashed up my back bedroom. He ran out of the house, and because I was worried and wanted him to be safe I rang the police.

I wish I hadn't. My son refused to forgive me and stopped having anything to do with me.

My son and his girlfriend live only ten minutes away from me, but I haven't seen them in about a year. If I do spot them his girlfriend covers my grandson's head so I can't see him, or if he is in his pushchair she turns it around so I can't see his face.

I hear he's the absolute double of my son so I'm always looking out for a child of that age, who looks like my boy. I have sent cards in the past for Christmas and birthdays, but they've been returned.

I've been told that there's no point in going to court, I wouldn't win the right to see my grandson. So what I do is put messages in the local paper. They're my tribute to him and they can't be returned. I also keep a memory box and I put cards and small presents in it for him. If I go away anywhere I buy a small token, so he knows in future years that I didn't forget him.

I've opened a bank account for him that I put money in each month. I hope one day I can let him know how much I care about him.

While Margaret's only hope is that her son and his girlfriend will relent and allow her to see her grandson, or that eventually Max will be old enough to make his own choice to see his grandparents, Kate has had to come to terms with the death of her daughter and the loss of the granddaughter she once thought would come to live with her.

Kate's story

Our daughter Sonia was an intensive care nurse and she met the father of her child at work.

They were together for just sixteen months when Sonia got pregnant, and when her daughter Maisie was five months old they split up.

The following July, when Maisie was just over a year, Sonia became ill. She was diagnosed with ovarian cancer, so she came to live with me and her father. The cancer was very aggressive and there was nothing that could be done. Sonia died aged just 31.

Sonia had wanted Maisie to live with us and for us to bring her up. Just before she passed away, a solicitor came round to see her and help her make a will. But before the will could be finalised and signed, Sonia became much worse and died very suddenly. She had been ill for just eight months, and Maisie was not yet two.

Maisie's father had always been very hostile towards Sonia and towards us. After she died, initially we were granted four days a week custody of Maisie, and her father got three. It lasted six months and then permanent residency had to be decided by the courts.

The child welfare officer came round and saw me and my husband with Maisie, and she also saw Maisie with her father. She concluded that Maisie needed all of us and said she would recommend joint custody, which I was very relieved about. But then all of a sudden she told me it couldn't be done. Maisie's father got residency and we were told we could see her every weekend.

Maisie and her father lived nearby, but all of a sudden, when Maisie was four, we got a letter from Devon saying that they'd moved there. Her father had met someone new and they were having another child.

We made the three-hour journey down there to see Maisie every three weeks, but since then her father has done everything in his power to stop our contact.

He started to claim that Maisie would come back in a terrible state after she'd seen us. The access dwindled to every six months' then to nothing; he stopped all contact.

I kept going back to court but I was told to step back because Maisie now has a new stepmother and they have to be allowed to bond.

They also said they were concerned about how the animosity between the adults affected the child. It seemed to us that he caused the animosity and it got the desired result.

We were given indirect contact, which meant we could send presents and cards every two months. We haven't seen Maisie for four years now.

I am devastated and I'm also angry at the system that has denied me contact with my daughter's child, my granddaughter, who used to be with us on a daily basis. My husband and I have suffered a double loss, and we worry about how it has affected Maisie, who lost her mother and then us. The whole system is flawed. I have *been fighting for seven years. Every door is slammed in your face. You can't get anyone to listen to you.*

Her father has never forgiven us for trying to take Maisie in the first place. But that was Sonia's dying wish. I am Maisie's history, I know about her mother. Richard only knew Sonia for less than two years before they split; how can he tell Maisie about her mother?

I'm pleased that she's in a family unit now, but to cut us out is absolutely cruel. I can't go back to court until Maisie is 12, in 2013.

Thank God for the Grandparents' Association, they've been fantastic. You don't feel so alone — you can talk to other people in the same situation.

Kate's story is heartbreaking. I know what it's like to lose a beloved daughter, and to lose your grandchild as well would be simply unbearable. Grandparents like Kate are fighting a brave battle to get the law changed, so that they aren't cut out of their grandchildren's lives at the whim of parents and stepparents. And stories like theirs highlight the need for parents to make their wills and sort out legal guardianship of their children, should anything happen to them.

Research shows that while young children can be happy in a situation in which they are being well looked after and loved, as they grow older a deep sense of loss, and the problems associated with this, can set in when their mum or dad is not there at those important times such as sports days, prizegiving, meeting a first boyfriend or girlfriend and getting married. And that's when grandparents can make a very real difference.

Thankfully some situations do turn out all right in the end, as Sue and George's stories show.

Sue's story

We have two daughters, Jan, who has two boys, and Marie, who has a daughter called Lauren. A few years ago my husband and I lost contact with Lauren, who was then seven, because of a dispute in the family.

Six years ago, Jan's younger son Peter, who was then eight, made an allegation about Lauren's husband, his Uncle Brian. They'd spent a lot of time together, as Marie and Jan would help each other out with childcare. The children were all very close.

But then Peter said this incident had happened, and at eight years old, why would you lie? How could you dream up something like that? Apparently Peter had stored this up for a long time because he didn't know what to do about it. Then one night his mum put him to bed and he started crying and crying and it all came out.

The police were called by a family friend and that's when the family was split. It was a terrible situation for my youngest daughter, because it was her husband who was being accused of abuse.

I was on holiday with my husband when it all blew up. We came home to hear that Brian had been arrested, and both our daughters were distraught. Marie was waiting for us on our doorstep saying, 'We've had the most dreadful week, Mum, it's been terrible . . . '

My Grandma

Grandmas house is always warm, but she talks forever.   Caitlin aged 10

I wish my Grandma lives closer.

Caitlin aged 10

She told us everything and we were shocked; then we had Jan on the phone.

We were in the middle, and we tried very hard to be supportive to them both.

My youngest daughter wanted us to get Peter to retract his statement, to say that nothing had ever happened. She was absolutely in denial about it, which you can understand, because it was her husband.

In court Brian was found not guilty, because there wasn't enough evidence. It was one of those situations, there were only two people there-my grandson Peter, and Brian. How can you prove anything? You can't. So Brian was found not guilty and he and Marie cut us off completely.

My husband died before the peace was made. Marie had been so close to her father. He desperately wanted to see her and kept saying, 'I do wish Marie would come.' But he died and it was too late. It was a most terrible thing to happen to any family.

For ages I tried everything to try and see Lauren but Marie wouldn't allow it. What happened had split the family down the middle.

Then someone recommended the Grand-parents' Association, so I rang them. They are strangers so you unburden yourself and you tell them the story. I found that very helpful.

I decided to hire a solicitor to try to get contact with my granddaughter. I knew the longer I left it the more she would forget me. We tried some mediation with Marie first but when that didn't work very well we went to the family court.

Lauren was 12 at the time and the emphasis was on her. Lauren had been interviewed and had said she didn't really want to see Nanny, because she couldn't remember me.

So I was granted indirect contact, which meant I could send letters or cards. I was hugely disappointed and felt distraught, but I had to accept that.

But when we came out of court I was in a side room with my solicitor when there was a knock on the door. Marie walked in and she said, 'Mum, you know I didn't want this to go this far. I want us to try and get back together again.'

And very slowly we did. We started to text one another. Then we met with the dogs, halfway, and we've gone on from there. They've been here for dinner and I've been over there.

Lauren is 13 now and is quite a young lady. She's very shy with me, because we've missed out on five years, but she's coming round slowly.

I have come to the conclusion that if you want to go forward, if you want to get things back — and I wanted my daughter and granddaughter back — then you've got to put a lid on things and say enough is enough and people make mistakes. That's what I'm doing and I think my husband would agree with me.

George's story

When grandparents are denied contact with their children's children, they feel lost, alone and confused. They often feel they have done something wrong and it's their fault. After our

187

daughter died and we temporarily lost good access to our two grandchildren, I founded a local support group because my wife and I didn't want anyone else to feel as isolated as we did.

My daughter Juliet died in 1997 at the age of 26. She was diagnosed with breast cancer during her pregnancy and she passed away after giving birth to her second daughter.

She'd had pains in her breast for a while but by the time cancer was diagnosed she was seven months pregnant and they could not give her chemotherapy. Instead she had a mastectomy and they gave the baby steroids and delivered her a month early. After baby Megan was born they took away Juliet's ovaries as well, but she told me herself that she knew she wasn't going to make it. She died two weeks later.

After we lost Juliet, Megan was in intensive care for eight weeks. Her elder sister Rachel, who was then two, stayed with us in the day and went home with my son-in-law Liam at night.

When Megan was strong enough to come home we cared for her and this arrangement went on for a few years. Liam worked in the day, then he'd come round for dinner and would take the girls back to their house.

When Megan was about three Liam met someone new and decided to move from Newcastle to Manchester with her and the girls. Suddenly our daily contact went to once a month. We knew we were on a slippery slope.

Every time we saw the kids they would come chasing after us asking, 'When are we coming back home?' We'd all come away crying.

Liam's wife viewed our time with the girls as a chore, as she had to bring them to meet us halfway. She'd try to cry off, complaining that the weather was bad or the girls were too tired.

I was worried about the future so I started to research our rights as grandparents, and in 1999 we went for a mediation session. There was a heated argument for a couple of hours but we managed to make an agreement that would be legally binding for several years — we would see the kids once a month at our agreed halfway point. We also agreed it would be flexible and we could write to each other to change it.

It did last quite well and eventually Liam split from his new wife when the girls were aged nine and seven. They stayed down in Manchester, but we got to see a lot more of the girls. Their dad agreed that they could come up any time they wanted to.

These days we see them all the time. Rachel is 16 and going to college and Megan is 14. She comes up regularly and she loves it.

I set up the group because when we were looking for help there was none. Lawyers cost a fortune and we were confused, we didn't know where to turn. We went down a lot of dead ends. We wanted to help guide people in the right direction.

Recently we have been lobbying and appealing to the House of Commons and the Scottish Parliament to consider a Charter for Grand-children. Grandparents are the biggest carers of children in the world but they don't have any legal rights whatsoever.

The Charter for Grandchildren says that children have the right to have their grandparents in their lives. Lots of children lose out badly if they don't have the protection and love of their grandparents. It is in a child's best interest to have a grandparent in their lives.

George is so right. Grandchildren deserve to have contact with their grandparents, and this shouldn't just be stopped because of a disagreement or change of circumstance.

Lucy is a grandmother who lost access to her two little grandsons and put her feelings of loss and grief into her poetry.

Lucy's story

I have two sons; one of my sons doesn't have any children and the other has three sons — two with his first wife, and another with his current partner.

When my son and his wife got divorced six years ago, his wife cut off all contact with us. So we haven't seen my grandsons Ryan and Charlie since then. Ryan was eight and Charlie was six; now they are 14 and 13. Before the split I had a lovely relationship with them, they'd come and stay with me and my second husband on their own, but if we saw them now we'd be strangers to them. There was a time — for about a year — when we didn't know where they were or where they were living and that was very distressing.

We tried to resolve the issue of access

amicably at first, but that didn't work. Then we tried to do it through the courts, and they were no help at all. We have no rights; the mother has all the rights. Even though my son pays maintenance and the family court has decreed that he can see the children once a fortnight his ex-wife won't allow it and the court doesn't enforce it.

Until fairly recently my son went to court twice a year to battle for access, but Ryan got very upset and my son decided that it just wasn't worth it. He doesn't talk about it any more, he just hopes his sons will get in touch and come and see him when they are older and can decide for themselves.

My son has a new partner and they have a five-year-old son, Harry. He means so much to me. He is such a mix of my other two grandsons — he has the looks of one of them and the personality of the other. Sometimes he does something or says something and I am reminded so vividly of Charlie and Ryan that it's a real kick to my insides.

I started dabbling in poetry about ten years ago and then when all this happened and I felt so angry and so powerless I found I needed a release, and that's when I started to write more seriously, and this year I published a book. There are so many people out there in my position . . . writing the poems did help me and I hope that they might help other people. I try to be hopeful. I decided I couldn't go on being angry; I had to be more positive . . . one day I hope I will see Ryan and Charlie again and I just

191

keep on thinking that, even though the hurt never goes away.

The courage Lucy and so many other grandparents have shown, and continue to show, in fighting for the right to see their grandchildren and refusing to lose heart is inspiring and encouraging. The more grandparents — and their supporters — who stand up to be counted and lobby for the law to change, the more pressure the authorities will feel, until eventually change will have to come about. Remember we are talking about the right just to see your grandchildren, not the right to influence the way they are brought up. It is wrong that children and grandparents should miss out on this vital family connection.

WHAT RIGHTS DO GRANDPARENTS HAVE?

Marilyn Stowe, a top family lawyer for over 25 years, is often in the position of having to explain to desperate grandparents seeking contact with their grandchildren that despite their blood relationship they have no automatic rights of contact with their grandchildren. If they want contact with their grandchildren and one or both parents refuses to grant it, they will need to apply to the court for help. Here are Marilyn's answers to some of the basic questions.

What is the process?

At the moment if grandparents want automatic access to their grandchildren, or in more extreme cases want their grandchildren to live with them, they must jump through two sets of legal hoops. First, they must obtain leave of the court to make their application. If successful, only then may they apply for an order.

To convince the court that they should have contact, the grandparents have to demonstrate that they are committed carers, that they have a good relationship with the grandchildren and that they have had frequent contact. They will need to prove that it is in the child's best interests for the court to deliver a contact order.

Assuming the court is willing to hear the grandparents' application an appointment with Children and Family Court Advisory and Support Service (CAFCASS) will often be necessary. The officer will look at the case and prepare a report to help the court come to a decision. If the report is favourable the court will very likely issue the contact order. In my experience most grandparents do get leave to apply.

What's the success rate?

There are no official figures for the success rate. Generally, it seems that the more acrimonious the case the less likely a good outcome for the grandparents. In practice, although grandparents may apply to the courts, the potential impact on their grandchildren and the non-recoverable costs involved mean that in many cases they simply give up.

What advice can you give grandparents?
Applying for a contact order through the courts is the worst-case scenario; it is preferable to resolve issues amicably and without the involvements of the courts.
1. Try to discuss matters with the child's parents at an early stage. Don't take sides or play the blame game. Make it clear that all you want is a reasonable, ongoing role in your grandchild's life.
2. When it comes to contact time, be realistic. Don't forget that the children may now have three households to move between — not just yours and theirs.
3. Don't use a court application as a way of getting back at your son — or daughter-in-law. Don't use your application as a way to reduce their time with their children, and don't use it as a weapon. The court will be highly critical of any person who appears to be abusing the process or using the law as a means to hurt the other parties.

Are there any changes in the law afoot?
Before the election the Conservatives vowed

to give new and improved legal rights to grandparents in England and Wales. They said they would change the law (the Children Act of 1989) to ensure grandparents do not lose contact with their grandchildren after a family separation, divorce or bereavement, and that grandparents would be put at the front of the custody queue if their grandchildren face being fostered or being taken into care.

As often happens, stirring pre-election talk fizzles out when the government actually gets into power. But the new government has taken a step forward; in June 2010 it launched a 'Childhood and Families Ministerial Task Force' to identify cost-effective policies. Deputy Prime Minister Nick Clegg said it was 'crazy' that millions of grandparents lost contact with grandchildren after a separation or divorce and he highlighted the need to give grandparents rights to 'step in' and care for grandchildren affected by family splits. The task force is expected to deliver its conclusions towards the end of 2010.

Marilyn would like to see the following changes:

First, I would scrap the rule that grandparents must first obtain leave of the court before they are even permitted to make an application for an order relating to grandchildren. I believe this is unnecessarily long-

winded, time consuming and expensive. Secondly, I would like to see the government move such cases away from the court system where possible, and put in place an alternative forum or tribunal, chaired by a trained mediator. This would provide a less formal setting for all, but its decisions would still be legally binding. It could bring families closer together, rather than pitting them against each other and driving them further apart.

In absorbing what lawyer Marilyn Stowe had to say, I was reminded of a very poignant situation I came across at a dinner a while ago. I found myself seated next to a judge whose speciality was family law. He and his wife proceeded to explain to me how they had tragically lost their only son to cancer two years earlier. But because of certain attitudes, their daughter-in-law had then cut off all contact with their only grandson, who used to be with them on a regular basis.

Even with all the judge's intelligence and inside knowledge of the law, he had been unable to negotiate any flexibility or leeway with their daughter-in-law. He and his wife were bereft on two levels, after losing their son, and then contact with their grandson.

When I rang to ask the judge if he would be prepared to outline his story for this book, I was so saddened to hear that he had died a few months earlier, from a sudden heart attack. Even though I had only been in his company for an evening, his story had stayed with me, and I felt deeply affected to learn that he had passed away with the extra burden of his great loss.

My granny makes delicious
cakes. She makes chocolate
cakes, coffee cakes and
amazing lemon cakes.
She also makes really
nice chicken pies.

By Mary-Anne aged 8

10

Grandparent Heroes

All loving grandparents would like to think they are heroes to their grandchildren. But this chapter is about two groups of grandparents I feel deserve particular appreciation — those who, through necessity, take over the upbringing of their grandchildren, and those who help to care for disabled and special needs grandchildren. In both cases there are many thousands of unsung heroes up and down the country, doing their absolute best to make the lives of their grandchildren happier, safer and more loving.

Grandparents who care for their grandchildren full-time, because the children's parents either can't or won't, give time, energy, love and support beyond all normal expectation. These are the grandparents who become what is known as 'kinship carers'. Most of these grandparents never expected, or wanted, to have to play the role of parents all over again in their later years, but in Britain today over 200,000 children are being brought up by their grandparents.

When the parents have drug or alcohol problems, mental health issues or are physically ill or disabled, grandparents are often asked to take over, and the process of taking on their grandchildren can be very sudden. Many have described a phone call or a knock on the door from social services, who say to them, 'If you can't take your grandchild, then they'll have to go into care.' In this situation most grandparents are going to say yes, and worry about the reality of the consequences later. But those consequences can be immense, not least because kinship carers operate under what is regarded as a voluntary arrangement, and so they are given less support, financial and otherwise, than professional foster parents.

Kinship carers are absolutely vital to the care system. There is a great shortage of foster carers, and sadly the pressure is increasing all the time. Since the 1970s there has been a big shift in children's care, so that where once 70 per cent of children in care were in residential care — children's homes, as we used to call them — now 70 per cent of children are in foster care. This is a recognition of the simple fact that children do better in families. And at any one time there are around 1,500 children waiting for adoption or long-term foster care. So there's a bigger role for extended family, and grandparents who will take over are invaluable.

Inevitably, then, the knock on the door to ask grandparents if they will take over is coming more and more often. And it can come as an enormous shock to grandparents to realise that their children can't cope as parents. They often don't realise how bad things are until that knock from social services comes, and they are unprepared for the enormous task of taking on grandchildren permanently. They find themselves having to adjust to the problems of their own child, and of course worrying hugely, while dealing with the needs of one or more children who have been through a distressing time.

When grandparents take over, they are appointed as the children's 'special guardian', under a Special Guardianship Order, which is issued by the courts. This is a private law order made under the Children Act 1989, intended for those children who cannot live with their birth parents and who would benefit from a legally secure placement. It's not as final as adoption, but a parent cannot apply to discharge it unless they have the permission of the court to do so.

Not only is there the change in circumstances to adjust to, with court visits to secure the Special Guardianship Order, but the cost to grandparents, in financial, emotional and practical terms, is enormous.

Yet it's so worthwhile. If grandparents can step in and care for their grandchildren when parents can't, the children benefit in many ways. They feel happier, they behave better, they thrive and do better at school than children in foster care, they are more stable — children in foster care are often moved several times — and they benefit from their own family and cultural identity. At the root of all this, of course, is the fact that they are loved by their grandparents, and that deep, abiding love gives them security.

Having said that, for many families it is not an easy situation. Although the youngest grandparent bringing up a grandchild in Britain today is 29, the oldest is 89, and for the older grandparents just coping physically can be a struggle. In some cases the children and grandparents help and look after each other, both sharing care and chores in order to manage.

The difficulties involved can be wide-ranging. For the grandparents there is the physical toll of parenting a second time around, the financial cost, and the challenge of coping with children who may be emotionally and behaviourally disturbed. The children will have lost their parents and may well have gone through a great deal of upheaval, uncertainty and distress, and this tends to show itself in insecure, clingy or sometimes aggressive and angry behaviour.

Children who go to live with their grandparents are often, understandably, full of resentment and grief about the loss of their parents; they feel abandoned and that their parents put their own needs first — even if the loss of the parent is through illness. The children may also be afraid that their grandparents, if they are elderly, will die. And they sometimes feel embarrassed about other children knowing they live with grandparents, so they try to keep it secret. The children know when their behaviour is difficult, but they find it hard to stop.

The Grandparents' Association recently produced a very moving report, *Children's Voices*, in which children living with their grandparents were asked about the reality of their lives. Forty children were asked about their experiences, and it became clear that for the children as well as the grandparents it was not an easy situation.

Many of the children said, 'Don't tell my friends from school, they'd laugh at me.' Others

202

felt their grandparents were too frail, or missed having someone to call Mum or Dad. Many said they didn't get pocket money, that their grandparents couldn't afford new clothes for them, and that they never had holidays. But despite all the problems, most were very loving towards their grandparents and wanted to be with them.

Both the children and grandparents feel, almost without exception, that there is not enough help and support available for them. They can feel very isolated, and yet these valiant families carry on, coping, loving one another and sticking together. I have the utmost admiration for them, and I hope the help they need will be forthcoming, as soon as possible. As my own daughter said in her journals, 'In the end, all you have is the love of your family.'

In the meantime there are support groups springing up around the country, and wonderful websites which offer support and the chance to share your story. There are also experts and advisors who can be found through the Grandparents' Association, who will listen and offer advice and information.

I have been struck time and time again by the selflessness of the grandparents who take on their grandchildren full-time.

Take Marsha, a mother to two daughters and two sons, who found herself a grandmother at the tender age of 38.

Marsha's story
My daughter Tania became a mother when she was just 18. She had just left college when she told

me she was pregnant. She wanted to have the baby, and I supported her. She had a gorgeous baby boy, who was absolutely perfect. It felt unreal being a grandmother, especially as I still had a 12-year-old son myself. But I loved it and my daughter used to bring her son, Jay, round to see me most days.

Tania seemed to be coping well for the first couple of years, until she met a boy who got her involved with drugs. She became dependent on heroin and I watched my bright, lovely girl become a hollow-eyed shadow of her former self. I did everything I could to get her off drugs, but she didn't stop.

Then one day she came and asked me to take Jay for her, because she couldn't look after him. I had seen it coming; I worried about him a lot and often had him to stay, because she wasn't caring for him properly. I got tough with her, told her she had to get her act together and face her responsibilities — she was a parent now, she had a child and he needed her. She had to make a choice, and I said I hoped it would be the right one.

Sadly it wasn't. Tania chose to go on using drugs, and social services took her son into care. They got in touch with me to ask whether I would take him, and of course I said yes. Jay was three. I couldn't leave that little boy in a care home, he was my flesh and blood and I had to take him. But I was angry with Tania; I hadn't planned on having another child. I was happy being a grand-mother, seeing my grandson and then handing him back. I didn't want the whole package again.

The courts appointed me Jay's special guardian and he came to live with me permanently. My son is now 15 and he loves Jay; the two of them get on very well. But my son will leave home in a few more years, and I'll still have another 10 or 15 years of looking after Jay. It's a lot to take on.

I have to admit, I did feel resentful for a while. I felt I'd lost my freedom. I had plans to go back to college and find a good job, and all that had to go on hold. But as I watched Jay becoming more confident and settled, I realised how important it was that I be there for him, to give him love and stability. Nothing is more important than a child's welfare.

I've joined a support group now. There are several other grandparents like me in my area, and it really helps to talk things over, share ideas or just have a moan to someone who understands.

When I hear stories like Marsha's I feel humbled. Until you are in the position of having to take over, you can't know what it would feel like, and the implications are immense. There is an unpaid, unappreciated army of grandparents out there, giving their grandchildren a second chance in life.

Ruth and Daniel's is an extraordinary story. They had brought up their son and daughter and were looking forward to retirement from their jobs in the retail industry when they found themselves having to take on not one but three grandchildren. Ruth tells the story.

Ruth and Daniel's story

Our son Dom isn't the most responsible man. He's gone through a few relationships, but we thought he'd settled down when he met Cindy and they moved into a house together. They had a little boy, Jamie, and we adored him. Everything seemed to be going well, until they had a second baby, a little girl called Karen. When she was just a few weeks old, Dom and Cindy split up. Cindy seemed to be suffering from postnatal depression, and she told Dom to leave and to take Jamie with him. The two of them came to live with us, and we hoped very much that the family might come back together, once Cindy was feeling better. But that didn't happen; the split became permanent, Dom met another girl and he and Jamie moved in with her. A few months later she was pregnant too.

In the meantime Cindy had become quite ill and baby Karen had been taken into care. We didn't hear about this for some time, but when we did we offered to have Karen to live with us. We couldn't bear the thought of our granddaughter being in care; it didn't look as though she would be going back to her mother; and in the meantime Dom's new relationship was in trouble, so he couldn't have Karen.

Then a social worker arrived on our doorstep and told us that Dom's new girlfriend was a known child abuser. They asked us to take Jamie, and said that the new baby would be taken straight into care unless we could have him or her too.

We found ourselves in an enormously difficult

My grandad is brilliant.
He has long, fluffy hair.
A lso a funny, loving smile
The thing I like of all
is he always offers me
his nice goodies

by Jasmine Bingley

age 7

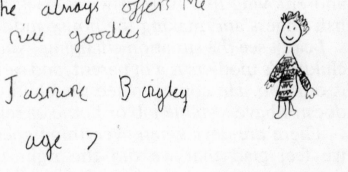

position. Our son had been irresponsible and produced three children he wasn't capable of looking after. We hadn't brought him up to behave like that, so there was a lot of soul-searching and wondering where we had gone wrong. And in the meantime there were three children — Dom's three children — needing a home. What could we do? We had to say yes.

We are now bringing up Jamie, Karen and the new baby, Lacey. They are lovely children and we do our absolute best for them. But we're in our sixties, and with three children under the age of six, to be honest, it's exhausting. We just hadn't planned on bringing up more children, we thought we'd done that and were looking forward to spending more time together, travelling and enjoying life. Instead we're back to nappies, fish fingers and making the house toddler-safe.

I can't see the situation changing. Neither of the children's mothers is a fit parent, and sadly, neither is our son. He comes to see the children, but he doesn't have a stable job or home or relationship.

There are days when everything goes well and we feel glad that we did the right thing. But there are other days when I feel close to tears with exhaustion, the children are playing up and everything just feels too hard. It can feel as though we've both walked into a nightmare, because this isn't just for a while, it's for as long as we're able to do it.

Jamie was four when he came to live with us, old enough to remember his mum and to feel very frightened and disturbed by all the changes in his life. So he has some pretty big tantrums, *and he needs lots of reassurance and security. My husband Daniel is wonderful with him, and will take him out in the garden and play with him for hours on end. But I do wonder how long we'll be able to manage a brand new family of three.*

No wonder I feel that grandparents like Marsha, Ruth and Daniel are heroic. It really is no exaggeration, when you see the changes they are having to make and the effort they put in. I hope that in the months and years to come their stories, and those of the many grandparents like them, will be heard far more widely, and that the help they so badly need will be given.

GRANDCHILDREN WITH SPECIAL NEEDS

The second group of grandparents I want to pay tribute to are those who help care for children with special needs.

The birth of a grandchild is such a big event. Learning that the longed-for child has physical or educational special needs can be a shock for the whole family, and it takes time to adjust, Expectations, plans and hopes may all have to change to encompass the needs of the child, and when parents are still reeling from the news and wondering how they will cope it is the grandparents who are often able to provide reassurance, support and comfort. At times like this their greater experience of life can be invaluable. They know that what seems like the end of the world may turn out to be a great blessing, and that a special needs child can bring immense joy to a family.

Beth was a young grandmother — she was only 43 when her first grandchild, Sarah, was born.

Beth's story

My daughter Alison was 23 and so excited about having a baby, but she began to feel that something was wrong when she was having a check-up in hospital. She felt the baby wasn't moving enough, but when she voiced her concerns they were dismissed by medical staff. She phoned me in a terribly upset state, and I did my best to reassure her that everything would be all right. But of course I was worried.

When Sarah was born she was adorable, and we couldn't see anything wrong. Alison and her husband Tim took her home, and as they live down the road I saw her most days.

As the weeks went past, Alison became more worried. Sarah wasn't trying to lift herself up, and at six months, when many babies are sitting, she was still lying down. At this point the doctors began to listen to Alison's concerns, and they went into overdrive, testing and measuring Sarah. They concluded that her head hadn't developed properly in the womb and that she had microcephaly, a syndrome in which the brain has stopped developing and the head is therefore smaller than usual. They told us that

Sarah would have problems, but we would have to wait to find out the extent of them.

It was terribly hard for Alison and Tim to learn that something was indeed wrong with Sarah, and they couldn't even know exactly what it might mean. The future seemed frightening and unclear and there were a lot of tears. My role at that stage was really to try to comfort and reassure my daughter. Sarah was a sweet baby and we all adored her. I knew she would always be loved and that we would cope, but it was hard to see my daughter so upset.

Sarah did everything more slowly than other children. She did eventually walk, but her cognitive skills weren't good and she was slow to speak. At 18 months she failed a key skills test — the pincer test — in which the child is asked to pick up tiny items from a table. A friend told me her disabled granddaughter had failed this test, and alarm bells went off for me. I suddenly realised that Sarah really did have serious problems, and might never lead an independent life. I agonised about whether to talk to Alison about my concerns, but eventually I did, because I felt more should be being done for Sarah.

When I told Alison of my concerns she cried for hours. It was very hard seeing her so distressed, but after that she and Tim pushed for more help and Sarah was sent to Great Ormond Street for a battery of tests.

Doctors there concluded that Sarah's brain damage had affected her muscles, her dexterity and her cognitive functioning. Until then we thought she would go to a normal school, but it

211

became clear that she wouldn't. It wasn't until she was older that we found out Sarah was also autistic, but by that time we had already coped with a battery of problems.

For me the joy of having my first grandchild was tempered by the pain of seeing my daughter so distressed, and the fear I felt for Sarah. There was a time when I felt terrified about how badly she was affected and how her life might turn out. And that fear became a barrier between me and my daughter. We had always been close, but I became afraid to get too close, or say too much, because of the fear we both felt.

As Sarah grew older, we all had to learn a lot about how to look after her. I was nervous at first, when she came to me and my husband for a night or a weekend. But I also felt it was a gift to be asked to look after this precious child. It meant a great deal to me. And we wanted to be able to give her parents respite.

When Sarah first spoke she wasn't very clear; I often couldn't understand what she was saying. My daughter always understood, but it took me time. I used to say, 'Grandma got that wrong. Aren't I silly? Will you say it again for me and let's see if I can understand.'

Sarah is 23 now and she lives in a house with three other special needs young adults. They have 24-hour support, it's called supported independent living and it's excellent — there is someone with her at all times and she has a good life.

Sarah needs a lot of help, but she is a loving and beautiful girl. She can use her mobile and calls us a lot. She makes us laugh, and I wouldn't be without her for the world. Her grandfather, Tom, is especially close to her; he adores her and has always spent a lot of time with her.

I'm also very proud of the way my daughter and her husband have coped. It was a shock when, as a young couple, their first baby had such major special needs. But they gave her everything she needed and never let her down.

Their second child, John, was born three years later and he is now 20 and a healthy, happy young man. My second daughter has had two children as well, so I have four grandchildren now, all of them gorgeous.

It was tough in the early days with Sarah, but she taught us a great deal and has always been so loving. We are blessed to have her.

Without the loving backup of Beth and her husband Tom, this family might have found it much harder to cope. Having grandparents there, ready to mop your tears, give you a hug and tell you everything will work out all right, is an enormous help and support.

It is natural to grieve when a child is born with disabilities — you will have feelings of loss or sadness for the child you were hoping for, and it takes time to adjust. But every grandparent of a disabled or special needs child I have spoken to has told me that for every challenge there are a dozen joys. And many families take the birth of a special needs child completely in their stride.

A good friend of mine, Jo, has ten grandchildren and she and her husband spend a lot of time with them. Their eldest grandchild,

Ian, was born with Down's Syndrome.

'We didn't have any inkling before,' Jo says. 'We only found out on the day he was born, so it was a very great surprise to us. Our daughter Susan has been an absolutely fantastic mum. We didn't discuss how we should treat Ian as such; we just always took our lead from Susan and treated him completely normally, as do the rest of the family. She said to me the other day, 'Of course you could have turned your back on him.' But we wouldn't have. We love Ian. He has never had any special treatment from us — I treat him just as I would any of our other grandchildren. And as with our other grandchildren, Ian has stayed with us and he's no bother at all. He just chats away and he loves to read and write and listen to music — he has brought so much to our lives.

'Ian will be 21 soon and although he lives with his parents and he's been to college they hope to get him into sheltered accommodation. It will be a positive step but it will mean him moving away from his home where he is looked after and protected. Of course I worry about that. But we'll all be there for him, as we always have been.'

Grandparents like Jo and Beth, and their sons and daughters, who cope with the extra needs of disabled children with such grace, love and dedication, are very special — as are those grandparents who take over the upbringing of their grandchildren to prevent them going into local authority care. Both these groups of grandparents are extraordinary, and they deserve all the support the rest of us can give.

At 76 grandpa walks the dog, works and plays tennis but he has a combover - I think it looks silly but he disagrees. Grandpa lives in London which is to fare away.

Ben aged 11

11

The Changing Shape of Families

All of us know that families come in every shape and size under the sun. Many of today's families are 'blended', which means they include step or adopted members, half-siblings and all kinds of other ways of being related to one another.

I like this, because it tells me that as a society we are becoming more tolerant and inclusive. Lots of children have brothers and sisters who are actually stepbrothers and stepsisters, or half-brothers and half-sisters, but children seldom bother with the qualifying 'step' or 'half', they simply feel they have more brothers and sisters, a bigger family, more playmates and, when things work out well, more security.

Our family has taken quite a few twists and turns over the years, but I feel that ultimately we are richer and stronger for it. Both Stephen and I are step-grandparents — he to my four grandsons, and I to his three grandsons and two granddaughters. We both love having nine grandchildren between us and, like most grandparents, feel incredibly proud of all of them.

Charlie and Gabriel's dad, Russ, has married again, and he and Sally, who has been a generous and really caring stepmother to the boys, now have two little daughters, the boy's half-sisters Tilly and Flora. Both the boys adored Tilly when

217

she arrived a couple of years ago, and they loved having a sister. She in turn also adored them, and that was very good for them. When little Flora arrived, this year, they felt just as excited. We have gorgeous photos of the boys playing with their little sisters, and it's easy to see that they feel protective and proud of these latest additions to the family circle.

Stephen and I relish seeing our clan grow. His youngest granddaughter, Lily, also arrived this year with her shock of black hair to join her big brothers: 15-year-old twins Jake and Billy, and Elliot who's 17. Then there's their cousin Elicia, who is 18 and has just started her nursing career.

Stephen's two sons Dominic (Elicia's dad) and Matthew (father to Elliot, the twins and now Lily) live in Cornwall with their families, so inevitably we don't see the children as often as we see mine, who live just up the road. But Elicia, Elliot and the twins are now old enough to travel up to London on their own, and we love it when they come to visit.

Elicia came not that long ago, and it was so lovely to have a girl about the place. I used to adore shopping trips with Caron, so I couldn't wait to go off shopping with Elicia to the Bluewater Complex near us in Kent and London's Oxford Street. Trust me, by the end of the trip we knew every single clothes shop along Oxford Street intimately!

Elicia's very pretty and very girly and loves dressing up. She was a tiny baby — just a pound and a half when she was born — and doctors worried that she might not grow properly, but she ended up being the tallest girl in her class. She has an incredibly caring nature, so nursing is a great career for her to pursue.

Elliot wants to join the forces as a sports instructor and recently Stephen took him to a reunion dinner of the 9th Parachute Regiment in London, with which he is associated. They both went off looking so handsome, in their dinner jackets and bow ties, and Elliot enjoyed meeting the old soldiers very much with all their inspirational stories to tell. Stephen became involved with the regiment, ironically, through tales about my dad's boyhood love of pigeon racing.

Dad always had a big loft with up to 90 or 100 birds, and during the war years (not that I remember, of course) we had a soldier permanently based in the loft in our back garden. The Paras used pigeons to send messages — much safer than Morse code — and my Dad received an award for his war effort. Stephen was fascinated by that because of the family connections, so he got in touch with them and now he regularly attends their get-togethers. He knew Elliot would be interested too; he's a disciplined young man who takes his physical training very seriously and would love a career in the navy.

The twins Jake and Billy came to stay recently as well. They're both very handsome, but difficult to tell apart! I still have to think hard when I see them. They are incredibly close to one another, but are developing slightly different personalities as they get older. One is now taller than the other too, and they tend to have different haircuts, so it's becoming easier to tell them apart. They're both brilliant cooks and are hands-on; they always offer to help when they come to stay, which is sometimes unusual in young people.

We are delighted when Stephen's grandchildren visit, and we see them when we go down to Cornwall — we still have the house that we bought in Fowey when Caron and Russ moved there 10 years ago. Nicest of all is when we manage to get both our families together. My two sons, Paul and Michael, get on extremely well with Stephen's sons, Dominic and Matthew. When they meet — which proportionately isn't that often, given the distances involved — there are bear hugs and back-slaps all round and they thoroughly enjoy catching up. Recently, we all met up for dinner in Fowey and it was so encouraging to see all these young adults chatting away at one end of the table comparing their daily lives — city life versus life by the sea in Cornwall. In the same way all our grandchildren get on well, even though my four grandsons are talkative and outgoing and Stephen's grandchildren can be a bit quieter and more reserved.

Inevitably Stephen has seen more of my grandchildren — and my children — than his own, simply because they live nearby and are around so often. So he's embraced being a step-grandparent wholeheartedly, and I thought I would hand over to him, at this point, and let him tell you what that has been like.

Stephen's story

I've been around Gloria's grandchildren since they were born — we got together shortly before Charlie's birth — so I know them extremely well and love them very much. In some senses, I've seen more of them than I've seen of my own grandchildren; it's just the way things are, simply because of the distances and the practicality involved. It takes at least five to six hours to get from our home in Kent to Cornwall, where they all live, while Gloria's children and grandchildren live less than an hour away.

My grandchildren call me Poppy and, despite seeing less of them, we have a very close bond. When they leave they say, 'We love you, Poppy,' and that means so much to me. Gloria's grandchildren call me Stevie, and though we have a good and close bond they don't pretend I'm their real grandfather, although I do represent that figure. Sadly one of their grandfathers is not with us any more, so I've done my best to fulfil that role in their lives, while being aware that there is a difference.

When Gloria's grandsons arrive, I'm always delighted to see them. They're more outgoing, talkative, noisy and demonstrative than my family are. They all love showbiz — of course they do, it's in their genes — and they love to sing, dance and generally entertain. They will throw their arms around you, while my grandchildren, on the other hand, are a bit quieter, more thoughtful and at times almost reserved by comparison. They show their feelings in more subtle ways. But I love that and

221

I feel very comfortable with them.

They even look very different — Gloria's grandsons are all blond, while my grandchildren are all dark.

Because we meet less often, when I see my grandchildren it takes us a little time to reconnect. It's a bit like booting up a computer. But once we get going we have a lovely time together. I love hearing about their lives — Elicia is beautiful, and made for nursing, and she's more bubbly and chatty than the boys. Elliot is so disciplined about his fitness regime, in preparation for becoming a sports instructor, and the twins, Jake and Billy, both box for Cornwall.

They've always been incredibly close and done everything together, and they're almost telepathic with one another. I remember when they were very little I handed Billy a biscuit. He carefully broke it in half and gave the other half to Jake. More recently, Jake lost a boxing match, on points, and Billy then fought the chap who beat Jake and knocked him out!

My grandchildren live a wonderful, healthy outdoor life in Cornwall. I hear about their everyday walks on the beach with their two dogs, and their trips on the boat the family acquired recently, which pulls a big doughnut behind it. The kids thrive on it all.

The truth is, I enjoy both sets of children and both ways of being. I enjoy the hurly-burly and razzmatazz when Gloria's grandsons are around, and I enjoy the calmer, more peaceful atmosphere when mine come to stay. Interestingly, on those rare occasions — usually

My grandad is not somba and grey he is Kind and funny... Hes fantastic.

My grate granny is wibbly and wobbly, she is very Kind and generous.

Noah age 9

Christmas or summer holidays — when we get both families in the same house, they all get on very well together. And I think Gloria and I both feel very blessed that we've got, between us, a big family and lots of gorgeous grandchildren who all like each other — we couldn't ask for more than that.

Stephen is absolutely right — although our two families are like chalk and cheese in so many ways, they get along brilliantly. They like each other's company when they meet up and we feel very fortunate that they do.

Just recently we took Charlie and Gabriel and two of their friends to Cornwall for a week, and it just happened to be regatta week in Fowey. It was wonderful to see all our grandchildren together, watching the Red Arrows give their annual display, and on Carnival night we enjoyed all the colourful and highly decorated floats going by, with the town band, the Carnival Queen, lots of children in fancy dress and everyone from grandparents to little children joining in. It was good old-fashioned fun.

I've really enjoyed getting to know Stephen's grandchildren, and he has always treated mine with great affection and warmth. It can't always have been easy for him, especially as we got together only a short while before Caron became ill, but he has been steadfast, there for all of us and utterly supportive throughout our time together.

So many other families have experiences like ours, where families are brought together through remarriage and have to learn to get along. And I think that most of the time, in most families, it works pretty well. But sadly the downside to blended families is separation and divorce. Most families today have had some experience of this — I can't think of many families I know where someone in the last couple of generations hasn't divorced.

Divorce isn't always, in itself, a bad thing. If a relationship is really not working and both parties are unhappy and have tried their best, then sometimes it's wise to move on, stay friends and find happiness elsewhere. However, as my lawyer once said to me, 'Keep the communication lines open because you can't put a bin-lid on years of marriage and there will always be births, deaths and marriages within the family.' But while this is the kind of separation or divorce most people would like to achieve, the reality can be harder. And those who are often affected most are the children.

Research now tells us that children often blame themselves when their parents divorce, no matter how much the parents tell the child it isn't their fault and that they're loved and will continue to see both their mum and their dad. And this is where grandparents can step in. They can be invaluable in giving the children continuity and, through that, reassurance and stability. One middle-aged man I know told me recently, 'My parents split up and we moved from house to house, but my grandfather's house was always the same. He never moved and when I went back there he would be just as I left him, sitting beside his wireless, fixing little bits of machinery, and happy to see me. Knowing that there was one place and one person in the world that wouldn't change gave me a rock to cling to in an unstable world. It was the biggest gift in my childhood.'

This man's lovely grandfather probably had no idea how important his role in his grandson's life was. They didn't meet that often, and they didn't talk that much, his grandson told me. But nonetheless he provided crucial stability in his grandson's uncertain world.

Grandparents play all kinds of roles when families break up. Recent evidence indicates that a father is more likely to stay in touch with his children after a separation if his mother is involved and has a connection with her grandchildren.

Grandparents can provide so much: continuity, advice, a listening ear, a reassuring hug or even a temporary roof for those whose lives are in turmoil. And grandparents — wise ones, anyway — will encourage warring parents to make peace and talk things out, for the sake of the children.

The most important rule, as every grandparent who has watched their adult child go through a breakup will know, is 'don't take sides'. Not always easy, but definitely necessary, especially when contact with the children is involved.

It may feel incredibly hard not to stick up for your son or daughter and criticise their partner — especially if the partner is the one doing the leaving. But it's worth remembering that every story has two sides, and it's important not to jump to conclusions or assume anything. Try to keep the lines of communication open with both sides, and be sympathetic in equal measures. Encourage them to talk and work out an agreement that means the children keep a strong link with both parents.

It is at times like this that parents are most likely to turn to grandparents for support — and that may be financial, practical and emotional.

It can be hard to know how much to step in. Should you take on extra childcare? Should you give them money? Should you be on the end of the phone whenever they ring up wanting to moan about the partner they've just parted from?

I think the answer is: all things in moderation. Every situation is different, and no grandparent wants to see their child and grandchildren suffer. But neither can you step in and rescue them, at least not without careful thought. Where possible it's better to encourage them to cope and sort things out for themselves, with you there as a listening ear, to give moral support and tell them how well they're doing and that everything will work out in the end.

One grandmother I know, Lesley, found it incredibly difficult to see her son deeply unhappy after his marriage ended.

'My son had been married for 18 years,' Lesley said. 'His wife suddenly announced she was leaving, and he was shocked — he hadn't realised anything was wrong. They had two little daughters and his wife took them and moved out.

'My son was heartbroken, and so depressed

that I worried about what he might do. He would ring me at times, in tears, and talk for hours. It's terribly hard when you love someone and can't fix it for them. But he was 42 and I knew he had to sort this out for himself. I suggested he see a counsellor, and he did. It helped him over the worst.

'I also encouraged him to go to mediation, and his wife agreed. They worked out an arrangement for him to have the girls half the time, and that helped him a great deal.

'For a long time he still hoped that he and his wife might get back together — until he discovered that she was involved with someone else. Then he knew she had moved on, and although he was terribly down for a few weeks he realised it was time to let go.

'Gradually he got his life back together and now, two years later, he has met someone else and is happier than he thought possible in those dark, post-breakup days.

'It wasn't easy for me to stay civil and polite to his ex, but I did, because of the girls, and because I reminded myself that you never know what has really gone on in other people's relationships. And I'm glad I did because I still see plenty of my granddaughters, and that is what matters.'

I think Lesley did all the right things in encouraging her son to go for counselling and mediation and in being there for him while refusing to condemn his ex. It can be a very delicate juggling act, managing relationships after a breakup!

I recently met Sam, a public figure, who told me that after the birth of his son he had also gone through a painful breakup, with the help and support of his mum.

When his girlfriend became pregnant it was unexpected, but Sam was thrilled when baby Peter was born, and doted on him from the start. However, despite making every effort for the sake of their child, the relationship didn't work out and he and Peter's mum parted when their son was a few months old.

Although things hadn't worked out with his girlfriend, Sam didn't want to walk away from his son. Sadly, though, relations with his ex were very strained, and the long, difficult battle to see his son involved a court case and affected the whole family deeply, including his mum, who filled in the rest of the story when I spoke to her.

'Sam didn't plan on being a dad, as it hadn't been the kind of long-term, stable relationship you would want before you have a child, but when Peter was born Sam adored him.

'We're a very big and a loving family. Sam's dad died when he was very young, so the last thing he wanted was for his son to grow up without a father. The relationship with Peter's mum, sadly, wasn't to be, but Sam wanted to be totally involved in his son's life and he fought hard for that right.

'We didn't see Peter for over a year, which was heartbreaking for Sam and the rest of our family. He was my first grandchild and I just wanted him to know us, and to know we loved him.

'During the long months when we saw very

little of him I had to open a drawer in my mind and put him away, because it felt too painful to live with. I still held him in my heart, but it was a desperate time, when even the best lawyers didn't seem able to help.

'It was a very difficult period for Sam, and all I could do was support him and encourage him to believe that things would work out and he would be able to see his son.

'Thankfully everything is all right now. Sam and his former girlfriend were able to resolve things. They are both good parents to Peter and they share his care. And I get to see my first treasured grandchild.

'Peter is walking and talking now and he and Sam adore each other. Sam often brings him over to see me and Sam's sisters, Maxine and Lauren, and we all spoil him rotten. He's a beautiful, intelligent little boy and he means the world to us.'

As Lesley's son and Sam both discovered, while separation is never easy, there is life afterwards. And while it's wonderful when parents stay happily together, if they find they must part, the children will cope — remember they are very resilient — as long as they have plenty of love and support in their lives. And who better to offer that than their grandparents?

My grandad's a farmer, he
shoot's rabbit's and he tell's
really good stories. And he's
always got his nose in a
news paper

by Callum Townsend
age 10

12

Avoid Nothing — Face Everything

There are times, in every family, when heartbreak and loss occur, and every family will deal with this in their own unique way.

For children their first experience of loss is often when a much-loved grandparent dies. At times like this, parents and grandparents will help children to understand, to deal with painful feelings and to move on, while treasuring the memory of the person who has gone. And, hard though this can be, when it is a grandparent it is in the natural order of life.

We grandparents — while hoping to stick around as long as possible — want to be the first to go. We've had our time on this earth and want those we leave behind to have just as long as we've had, and hopefully longer. We don't mind dying first, because we should, and wise grandparents will let their children and grand-children know this, so that when the time comes they will have no need to feel guilty or to grieve too much.

With any luck we can leave behind us a legacy of happy memories. I would love my children and grandchildren to miss me — of course I would. I'd love to think they will laugh and tell funny stories about the silly things we used to get up to, and carry on gathering together, just as

233

I've always loved our family to do. I'd certainly like them to sing, dance and celebrate at my funeral.

The passing of a grandparent, while sad, is not a tragedy. But the death of younger family members is truly tragic, and affects the whole family very deeply indeed.

Since my daughter Caron died, I have spoken to many people who have lost their children and grandchildren. Such a loss leaves a void that is impossible to fill; nor would you want to. I call it the black hole.

The passing of time may blunt the sharper edges of grief, but that grief will never go away. You simply find ways to learn to live with it. In my own case, working hard and keeping busy have helped. It may not be everyone's way of coping, but keeping my head busy helped me. But most of all, my grandchildren have been an enormous source of comfort and have given me a reason to carry on.

Throughout the years that Caron was ill, when she and her family moved first to Cornwall and then to Australia, I wanted our home in Sevenoaks to be a permanent and unchanging fixture in the children's lives. I wanted them to know that they would always come back there, to think of it as another home, just as my grandparents' homes were for me, and to associate it with comfort, safety and peace.

This didn't just work one way. Having my grandsons around throughout Caron's illness gave me great comfort. Their beauty and brightness, their straightforward optimism each day, their sense of fun, their loving hugs and their energy made a world of difference.

I wanted so much to be a good grandmother, but in the end it was the boys who led the way, as they have so often, and showed me what they needed: trust, reliability, discretion, laughter, stability and patience are all in there. I don't always manage all of them, but I do my best. And we grandparents are wise enough to know that our best is all we can do. It's enough to be good enough.

Through those years, alongside my worry and sadness over my daughter's health, I was also deeply concerned for my grandsons, and the impact on them. They loved and adored their mum, and they needed her. Caron idolised them and fought so hard to forever be there for them, she always said she never wanted her boys to grow up without their mum, but inevitably the illness and the medical treatment involved took their toll and she sometimes became so tired and simply couldn't run around and do the things most young mothers do. I remember she wrote to Gabriel in her journal, 'I may not be able to trampoline with you, ride bikes or roller-skate, but I can read to you, paint and draw with you, watch a movie with you and chat.' She gave them some very special memories, and what has turned out to be an exceptionally solid base.

As you can imagine, for me it was a hugely painful, worrying and deeply anxious time. I didn't want to lose my daughter and I didn't want my grandsons to lose their mother. I so often felt helpless at my inability to change fate, I wanted to shout at the Gods and pray they save her. Instead I did my best to hide my heartbreak and did what I could, and that, often, was simply to be there for the boys.

When Caron died, after seven years spent fighting breast cancer, she was just 41. And even though we had known she was very ill, her death still came as a terrible shock. Caron had always been so positive, so determined to beat her illness, that we all believed she would, right to the end. It just didn't seem possible that our vibrant, beautiful girl would not win her battle.

The day she died, at our home in Sevenoaks, I honestly didn't know how I could or would go on. How would I ever get up, wash, dress, work, cook, talk, laugh or function in the world again, under the weight of a loss that felt utterly all-encompassing?

Only those who have watched a precious, cherished child die can know the pain it brings. I would have taken Caron's place and pain at any time. I felt my heart and my soul break into a million pieces and knew they would never be put back together again. I sat beside her, holding her hand, willing her to stay, or to take me instead.

I hadn't even noticed the doctor arrive, but as Russ and I looked at one another and said, 'How will we tell the children?' the doctor took us aside and said, 'You watch, the children will lead you . . . ' Those were powerful words, and almost hard to believe, but they turned out to be so true. Charlie, who was then ten, and Gabriel, who was seven, did show us the way.

At the time, in the midst of the disabling

236

reality of losing Caron, we were so worried and anxious for Charlie and Gabriel. They were downstairs and Michael, my younger son, went down to give them a cuddle. Charlie said, 'Is Mummy going to wake up?' and Michael said, 'I don't think so, darling.' But of course the boys didn't really understand. None of us really understood and later that day my heart broke all over again when I found Gabriel knocking on the door of the bedroom where Caron still lay and saying, 'Wake up, Mummy, you've had enough rest now.'

I wondered then how these two gorgeous and innocent children would manage without their mum. Luckily they have a fantastic father in Russ, and a big family who all love them, and they seem to have coped extraordinarily well.

The day that Caron died, however, we were all so numb with grief, so lost and so bewildered, that we sat and watched tributes to her on the television that evening. Looking back we often wonder how we did that, but we felt drawn, almost magnetically, to the opportunity to see life in Caron and see her laugh and chat, even though it was only on the television screen. It was as if we clung to every shred of her being. It only compounded our grief and made it all seem even more unreal, but we just didn't know what to do with ourselves.

What got us through was having to be there for the boys. The only thing that got me up the next day was the knowledge that two little boys would need breakfast and would have to be kept occupied for the day.

I was very fortunate, because Russ and the boys stayed with Stephen and me in Sevenoaks for almost three months after Caron died. I think we all got through that period by feeling our way, leaning on each other and gradually beginning to make plans and decisions again. Always, at every point, we were led by the children.

Children experience grief differently to adults. They appear to dip in and out of it, and can seem terribly sad one minute, and quite bright and positive the next. They don't stay down, and always return to normal life in between bouts of sadness. One moment they would say, 'I miss Mummy,' and the next they would run off to play in the garden or bounce on the trampoline. Theirs was a wonderful example for us to follow. Although all the 'normal' things we did felt anything but, and we functioned like automatons for a long time, the very fact of having to prepare meals and keep the children in some kind of routine helped. We began to realise how right our GP had been when he said the children would lead us.

Caron died during the Easter holidays, but when school began again the boys were still with me in Sevenoaks. It seemed more important that they stay with us and have some time to heal than for Russ to rush back to Cornwall and throw them back into school life. The other children at school would have no concept of what the boys had been through in the holidays and we felt it might be too much for the boys to cope with so soon. So they stayed with us and we spent a great deal of time together.

While she was ill, I promised Caron that I would always look after her boys. When she asked me, it was one of the very few references she ever made to the fact that she might not make it. Mostly she planned for life, not death, but at that moment she was very serious, and I was so touched and honoured to be asked. I promised her that I would always look out for them and do my best for them, and keeping that promise has given me great purpose over the past six and a half years.

A few weeks after Caron died, Russ ventured back to work. He had always kept in touch with his company by phone and online and was still a partner in the business, but going back into the office was yet another of the hurdles on the road back to 'normal' life that had to be faced.

Russ and Caron and their boys had been abroad for some time, first for just over two years in Australia and then, in the last three weeks before her death, in Switzerland. Stephen and I had been there with them, as Caron underwent treatment in a Swiss clinic. When we realised Caron was deteriorating fast, Russ had driven through the night to get her back to England, while Stephen and I flew ahead of them to be waiting, so that we could care for her in the safety and peace of our home. We knew she was very ill, but we had no idea just how ill until she arrived home with Russ, just after midnight, when Russ and Stephen had to carry her from the car as her body had seized up during the long drive.

Caron managed a cup of tea, in her favourite

spotty cup which had belonged to her grand-mother, sitting at the kitchen table — something she had looked forward to and talked about for a long time. Unbelievably, and to this day still impossible to grasp, she died only hours later, as Russ, Michael and I sat beside her, holding her hand and clinging to her with every fibre of our being.

In the following days and weeks, most of life was a daze of trying to cope with daily life. While Russ readjusted to the world of work, I remained at home with the boys, doing my best to give them stability at a time of utter emotional turmoil.

During that period Cliff Richard, a family friend for many years, who was deeply fond of Caron, offered us his house in Portugal for a break. The boys did all kinds of fun things there: go-karting, swimming, playing tennis and riding mini motorbikes. They laughed and seemed care-free, though we knew they were still very much on fragile ground and we were still functioning on 100 per cent autopilot.

In early July, 12 weeks or so after Caron died, Russ took the boys back to their home in Cornwall. He and Caron had moved there before they went to Australia, and he needed to take the boys back. After all, their things were there, and they wanted to see their friends and needed to go to school and try to pick up some of the threads of their lives. I understood that, and supported it, but it was a huge wrench when they went.

I am so glad that I was able to be with Russ

and the boys for those weeks, and that after that I was always included in the boys' lives and was able to be a link for them with their mother.

I believe that when a momentous life-changing event like this happens, the family structure is so vital. It is a time when the connections and support in the family are truly necessary and, for the children's sake, need to be maintained.

Recently I met a woman who told me her daughter had died a year earlier, and within four months her son-in-law had remarried. She had found that hard to accept and they had virtually lost contact, because she didn't want to have to deal with his new wife. But as a result she wasn't able to see her grandchildren any more. I urged her to put conflict and her hurt feelings aside and find a way to build bridges again, because her grandchildren need her and she needs them. The children have to come first, however hard that is for the adults.

In the first year after we lost Caron I found every anniversary agonisingly painful. Shortly before she died we celebrated Mother's Day — our first together for three years, and we spent it, just the two of us, in the Swiss Alps, scoffing apple strudel and talking, as we always did. A week or two later it was my birthday, and Caron gave me a painting, of tulips, that she had done in Australia and taken with her to Switzerland to give me. It was beautiful, and so typical of her that, ill as she was, she still insisted on organising a lovely birthday celebration for me — as she had always done.

She died only three days later, and as these

241

anniversaries came round again it was agonisingly difficult. My generous and very thoughtful sons, Michael and Paul, knew how hard it would be, and the following Mother's Day they turned up together with a bag of shopping and insisted on cooking me dinner, which included Paul's famous pavlova, something he hadn't made since his teens. I was so touched.

But before that there was Christmas to get through — a time that Caron had always delighted in. I didn't know how I would manage to cope with that first Christmas, but in the end I decided that having all my grandchildren around me would be the best way. So I asked Russ to bring the boys and Paul and Sandy to bring their boys, and of course Michael to come too. Both Michael and Paul were extremely kind, understanding and thoughtful in the aftermath of Caron's death, as Russ was. In the midst of their own loss and grief they didn't hesitate to say yes to my Christmas needs. Maybe they needed it as much as I did.

On Christmas Eve it was desperately sad to see Russ wrapping the boys' presents, when in my head I had vivid memories of the year before, in Australia, with Russ and Caron wrapping them together. Then, just before bedtime, the four little boys — Charlie, Jake, Gabriel and Beau — looked out of the window and swore they could see Santa coming on his sledge. There was a light twinkling in the sky — more than likely a plane heading for nearby Gatwick — and the boys were beside themselves with excitement. We told them he wouldn't stop if they weren't in bed, so they raced off to put out their stockings. I've never seen four boys get into bed so fast! The next morning we watched them, happy and excited, opening their presents, and it made Christmas bearable.

★ ★ ★

In the months after Caron's death I felt I wanted to do something in her name that would bring benefit to others. Caron, like so many people, was such a positive, courageous person, and she had enormous curiosity and an adventurous spirit. I wanted to celebrate those qualities in something truly worthwhile to counteract such a well of loss. I talked to Russ, Paul and Michael, and they felt the same way, so on what would have been Caron's birthday, 5 October 2004, we launched the Caron Keating Foundation at the Savoy Hotel in London.

We decided not to do bricks and mortar and huge research projects, because that takes millions of pounds. Ours would be family run and help lots of small and worthwhile cancer projects all over Britain.

The idea of the Foundation is to raise funds to help those battling cancer — and to include all kinds of cancer charities, not just those connected with breast cancer, from which Caron had died. I am the administrator of the Foundation, and run it on a daily basis, with the help of a part-time secretary. That is our only overhead, so we know that all the money we raise goes to the cancer charities. It is a privilege for me, and part of my own healing, to do something positive, to assist other people against the negativity of losing Caron.

Caron always had an interest in complementary therapies, and during her illness, alongside all the orthodox treatments she received, she researched and explored and tried out many complementary treatments. Although they didn't save her life we believe they may have extended it and helped her to cope with the pain. I don't doubt that some of these treatments and therapies helped her, both physically and spiritually. She found calm and peace and felt supported, and that meant a great deal to her, and to those of us who loved her. So one of our aims is to encourage the orthodox and the complementary to work together, in healing.

Since its inception the Foundation has raised nearly £3 million, and it has been a real joy to give this money to a wide range of worthwhile cancer organisations and we now have a number of Caron Keating treatment rooms in different parts of the country.

I think Caron would be proud of what we have tried to do in her name and would be astonished at the support and help we get from so many different people all over the country.

We give lots of smaller grants to cancer support services, as well as helping to purchase pieces of machinery which diagnose cancer faster. And we support some of the work being done, for instance a Northern Ireland radiographer from Action Cancer who screens young women, outside the NHS, using a mobile 'Big

Bus' unit. What's marvellous about it is that it can travel round various locations in Northern Ireland, for example a factory yard or a housing estate. They screen women, and by the time they have re-dressed and had a cup of tea the result of their mammogram can be beamed back from their HQ. Bearing in mind that Caron was only in her thirties when she was diagnosed, this seems an especially apt project to support.

When we first launched the Foundation, Caron's boys were still very young, but we have always told them about it and as they've grown older they have become increasingly involved.

This brings me enormous joy, because Caron's boys are the future. I look at them and know that her spirit is alive. I often heard my grandmother talking about the spirit living on, but when I was young I didn't really know what that meant. Now I do, because I see so much of Caron in them. They are both so like her, in their looks, in their adventurous spirits, in their love of humour, song, dance and adventure, and in their ability to make an everyday event into a celebration.

I have always believed that 'avoid nothing, face everything' is the best approach to the difficult and painful things in life, so I have been very honest with the boys in talking about their mother, her life and her illness. After all, my favourite adage is, 'People never die if they live on the lips of the living.' And I wanted the boys to get involved with the Foundation to help them feel that real good has come from the sadness of their mum's death.

One of my proudest moments of realisation that the boys understand the idea of the Foundation was when Charlie was only 12. He told me that at school he was asked to write an essay about what he would do as a fundraiser. He wrote about a sports day and said that he would give the proceeds to the Caron Keating Foundation. When I read the essay it brought tears to my eyes. The Foundation is just one strand of the powerful connection he and Gabriel have with their mother, and I think it's constructive for them to know how much their mum was cared for and respected and what we try to do in her name.

In recent years the boys have come with me to some of the bigger fundraising events and the fun occasions organised by, or in the name of, the Foundation. One of these took place last year. It was Women of Rock, organised by the Hard Rock Café and held in the Albert Hall. Hard Rock is a family-based structure and they support the Foundation every year with fund-raising events in Caron's birth month, October. They put in a huge amount of work and effort on our behalf, which is so appreciated.

For the past four years Hard Rock have held fundraising music events at their cafés during the month of Pinktober, but Women of Rock was held for the first time in October 2009 and it was a sensational night. The idea was to have women on stage, performing for other strong women dealing with breast cancer. We were lucky enough to have appearances from stars including Joss Stone, Jamelia, Bonnie Tyler,

Melanie C, Escala, Bananarama, Sharon Corr, Nerina Pallot, Tulisa, the cast of the stage musical *Mamma Mia!* and many more. It was so successful that Hard Rock decided to hold it again this year, at the O2 Centre.

At the Albert Hall last year Charlie and Gabriel, their friends and their cousins Jake and Beau occupied the whole front row, and they had fabulous fun in the middle of all that rock music. It was so good for them to see what was being done in their mother's name (and in the case of Jake and Beau, their aunt) and to know how much she was respected and valued. At the end of the show Charlie and Gabriel came on stage and presented me with flowers. I hadn't known they were going to do that, and it was quite a moment!

Another of our successful annual fundraising events is Strictly Tea Dancing, which we hold at the Langham Hotel in London, opposite the BBC in Portland Place. The idea is to have a tea dance, with all the fattening goodies to eat (sticky buns are definitely on the menus!), and some of the stars of the BBC's *Strictly Come Dancing*, to give demos and to dance with guests. You can imagine how popular that is! The boys came along to the event with their friends and they had a whale of a time.

Under the banner of the Variety Club of Great Britain, there's also a Caron Keating Award for young talent which has been awarded every year since Caron died, and as Charlie and Gabriel get older the hope is that they will soon be involved in the presentation of the Award.

The other event that was very memorable was a reception held at 10 Downing Street and hosted by the then Prime Minister's wife, Sarah Brown. I hadn't known that Sarah was at Bristol University at the same time as Caron and when we met on another occasion, she offered to host a reception for Caron's Foundation, as a thankyou to some of the people who have given so generously. Sarah herself, of course, knows what it's like to lose a child, so her offer was extremely thoughtful and apt. Many well-known supporters of the Foundation came along, and it was invaluable in raising the Foundation's profile. Sarah Brown called it an 'ongoing celebration of Caron'. I had taken Charlie and Gabriel along, and I was so pleased that they were able to see such a lovely tribute to their mother. Jake and Beau were also there and I've got pictures of them all standing on the doorstep of Number Ten. Definitely one for the family album!

Every year on Mother's Day, in March, and again on Caron's birthday in October, we take the boys to visit her grave. She is buried in the churchyard of St Peter's, the church at Hever Castle, where she was married.

Let's face it, many people simply don't like going to the graveyard, and the last thing we want is for it to be a dread, or an over-sad occasion, so to try to soften it we make it a family outing. The whole family meets for lunch in the King Henry VIII pub across the road, where the adults catch up while the children play. Then we go over to see Caron, taking balloons and flowers and cards (what the man who looks after the graveyard thinks, I'll never know). The boys write her a card each and they are almost exactly the same as if she was alive but in another place — just normal, chatty cards. Gabriel often used to make little gifts and treats at school and then leave them at her graveside.

Recently Paul found some amazing rockets which shoot 150 feet up into the air. We all wrote messages to Caron and tied them to the rockets before we launched them in a nearby field. So strange as it may seeem we make it a fun occasion to celebrate Caron's life.

Many of Caron's friends leave gifts and tokens at her grave. For example, Richard Madeley, a very good friend to Caron and Russ, left a bottle of champagne there when he got a new contract and we often find little gifts and notes left by people who knew and admired her.

Caron's boys are the miracle she has left us, and I know they are enormously proud of her, as we are of them. I hope that one day they will take over the running of her Foundation and keep it going, so that the blessings that she left behind will continue to multiply — never forgetting for one single second, of course, the thousands of people who help us raise valuable funds so that we in turn may help others all over the country.

My Nana!

My Nana is the most loveliest, kindest, friendliest Nana you could ever find. But she's ALWAYS going on cruises!

By: Laura Ann, age 11.

Epilogue

Keeping Up With the Growing Years

My grandsons are growing up so fast that it always gives me a shock when I see how tall they are! Three of them are teenagers now — Charlie is 16, Jake 15, Gabriel almost 14 and Beau, the youngest, is 12, so it won't be long before I've got four teenage grandsons. And Stephen's boys are all teenagers and over six feet tall.

It's been a real joy and experience watching them grow, develop their separate interests and become their own people, with their various characteristics. All grandparents will have their own stories to tell and their separate observations to make, but here are a few of mine.

Charlie is almost ready to fly the nest. He's tall, very good-looking (actually they all are — total bias aside! Those girls are already showing a great deal of interest) and confident, with a fantastic sense of humour. He has just started to board for his sixth-form years, while he concentrates on his A-levels. He's chosen English Literature, History, Photography and Media Studies. Now there's a surprise! As his father, mother, grandfather and grandmother as well as his stepmother all have a background in television, it's not surprising he's leaning towards the media for his career. But Charlie says he'd rather be behind the cameras, like his grandfather Don, who was a TV producer

251

and director, than in front of them. He's passionate about film and he's lucky to have the scope of the school's own editing facilities and their TV and photographic studios, so he's very excited by his new environment.

Like all of my other grandsons, who seem to have it in their genes, Charlie is musical; he writes songs, sings, and plays the guitar and drums, and does the odd bit of crazy dancing.

Jake is a fantastic sportsman — he loves rugby and is always in his school's A team; he's also a great cricket player and a strong swimmer. He changed schools last year and won a sports and music scholarship to his new school, which made us all extremely proud. He's a very talented musician and plays piano and guitar.

Jake may not thank me for saying this, but it's been observed that there are times when he looks particularly like me. I can't claim to have natural blonde hair like him, but Paul was looking at a picture of the two of us recently and laughing as he said, 'Goodness the two of you look so alike.'

Jake and Beau's mum Sandy is a great champion of sports for boys, and she takes them all over the place to matches and practice sessions. In the holidays they're often to be found at some big adventure course, climbing rocks, surfing in Cornwall or skiing in northern France.

Gabriel, since he was a small child, has the gift of the gab. When the boys put on shows he's inevitably the Master of Ceremonies, introducing and making the announcements. He always asks very original and thoughtful questions, so there's no doubt in my mind that he could be a television presenter and interviewer if he wanted to. I often joke that I'll start ringing him before a tricky interview to see what questions he would ask! However, at 13 he's got lots of time to decide what he wants to do. He's done very well in his exams and will go on to board in the sixth form like Charlie.

I'm sure it must have been a big wrench for Gabriel when Charlie went away to school. They had always been together through everything that has happened in recent years. But when I ask Gabriel, does he miss his brother, he says, with great bravado, that he now has the place to himself during the week when Charlie is away. And of course he has his two baby sisters at home with him, and plenty of friends around.

Beau is a keen sportsman, like his big brother, and he's also a very talented musician — he plays the saxophone and is a brilliant drummer. His dad, Paul, took to the drums in a big way as a small boy, and I have vivid memories of Paul washing neighbours' cars to earn the money to buy a cymbal or snare drum. I remember hauling his drum kit around from place to place in the car. Now Paul does that for Beau, who is so talented that when I took him into a music shop recently and he began to play one of the drum kits, another customer said to me, 'I was going to have a go myself, but after hearing your grandson I wouldn't dare!' He's such a good drummer that older boys are always asking him to go along and play with them at gigs on the weekends.

Beau is also extremely good with his hands and makes wonderful things. He is a talented artist and cartoonist and he has a wickedly mischievous streak and constantly makes us scream with laughter.

Not long ago Beau invited Stephen and me to his school's grandparents' day. I adore those days, alongside many other grandparents, when the children show us around the school and then give us tea. During tea every child did something to entertain us. To our surprise, as he had just taken up the instrument, Beau played an absolutely wonderful saxophone solo of the Pink Panther theme tune, and then played those drums with the orchestra. We were immensely proud of him, but it was the same for all of us — there were dozens of grandparents in the room with us and a great deal of pride and preening going on!

Gabriel also invited us to his school, for their community day, and it was another delightful and totally memorable time. The children served tea and showed us around and it was lovely to see how proud they were of their school and their families. One of the great thrills and revelations as a parent or a grandparent is seeing children develop and observing the unique adult emerging in each of them, as well as the echoes of their parents. My grandsons are their own individual selves, and yet I can also see so much of Paul in his boys and Caron in hers.

Gabriel is the one who looks most like her. Two of the many photographs I keep beside my telephone at home remind me just how similar

Gabriel and Caron are. The first is a photo of Gabriel, aged seven, sitting on the floor cuddling a puppy. The second is of Caron, at the same age, sitting on the floor cuddling her doll Susan. Apart from their hair and clothes, you would swear it was the same child in both photos. They are so alike.

Charlie has definitely inherited Caron's quirky sense of humour. She was always making me laugh with a wicked comment or a sideways take on life, and Charlie is exactly the same. I'll say to him, 'When are we going to such and such?' and he'll say, straight-faced, 'The 32nd of August.' I have to pause for a moment before I twig and then can't help laughing. Everything is a tease and everything seems fun.

Both boys are avid readers, as Caron was. She was never without a book in her hand if she had a five-minute break or had to wait for a bus, and the boys are the same. Charlie was reading Harry Potter at six and Gabriel had read the whole Harry Potter series five times over by the time he turned 12.

As I mentioned earlier, it's interesting to watch the spirit carrying on. It's not the way I would have liked it to come about, but at the same time it is a strange kind of privilege to witness Caron's spirit being carried on in such an evident and powerful way in her boys. It's something which brings me a huge amount of comfort and, to a degree, healing.

All four boys appear to be born entertainers, and with their background it's not really surprising. I've got so many wonderful memories of the shows they put on in our conservatory at home, with Stephen and me, their besotted audience, lapping up every minute.

Our grandsons are a constant source of happiness and intrigue for me. I love being with them, listening to them talking and hearing about their lives. Sometimes when I'm driving and all four boys are in the back, I enjoy hearing their latest bits of chat and their naughty lavatorial school jokes.

Mind you, they can be really wicked when it comes to playing pranks on me. Not long ago we were in the pub in Hever, opposite the churchyard where Caron is. We had been to visit her and were having tea in the pub before going home. The boys kept running in and asking me for pound coins and I doled them out, thinking they were playing on some sort of slot machine. At one point a man walked past me and said with a twinkle, 'Your boys are certainly having fun,' but I kind of dismissed it, as I was deep in conversation with Paul.

When we left the pub a little while later we went outside to find my car covered in yellow balloons. Well, I thought they were yellow balloons. They turned out to be yellow condoms, which the boys had bought from the vending machine in the gents, then blown up and stuck all over my car! The four of them thought it was the funniest thing ever, and fell about laughing.

All four of the boys are extremely outgoing, talkative, confident and affectionate. My own family in Ireland were very huggy people. Charlie may be 16 and tower above me, but he still gives me a lovely hug when we get together, and I've seen him leap on his dad for that big bear-hug. A warning though — in those early teens public hugging becomes a bit of a no-no, particularly when you're picking them up from school. So I used to say, 'I want that hug and kiss once we're inside the car.' What is it they say? We should all have seven hugs every day.

Like other kids their age they live on their mobiles and iPods and gadgets of one sort or another. But they're also polite and friendly and more than able to hold their own in a thoughtful or topical conversation. Their parents have done a fantastic job of bringing them up and are justly proud of all of them.

What I've learned, as they've grown, is just how different being a grandmother to older youngsters is from being a grandparent to little ones. Whereas when they were small I could cuddle them, draw and paint with them, read them stories and play with them and their idea of heaven was to dip into my goodie cupboard, now their needs are a bit more sophisticated. (Although, come to think of it, they do still love the goodie cupboard!)

It's a question of going with their interests and finding common ground to keep communication flowing. You have to learn to do new things with them, particularly as a woman with boys. I can't kick a football or be a match for them at cricket, as grandfathers can, but I can go tenpin bowling, get tickets to rock concerts or take them to the theatre.

Just to keep in touch I'll often ring and say,

'Hi, this is Nana, I'm just calling to say hello,' and they'll send me a text in reply. I read their texts, but I don't text back, I prefer to have a chat. A bit old-fashioned, I know, but I always think we grandmothers are allowed that prerogative.

Now that they're older we try to introduce them to new experiences, and take them to new places which they will always remember. Who doesn't recall their first visit to New York or Paris? When my children were younger I kept well up on the music and charts and at the time I became a fairly cool mum because I often interviewed their pop icons. Caron was potty about David Essex and Rod Stewart and when I introduced them at the television studios it was one of the few times I saw her lost for words.

I'm doing my best to try to be a cool grandmother as well. Not long ago Charlie was rather keen on Diana Vickers, one of the girls who appeared on *The X Factor*. Diana didn't win, but she was very popular and went on to top the charts and appear in the West End in the musical *Little Voice*. We all went to see it and then went backstage to meet her. She was very sweet and, just like his mum before him, Charlie was temporarily tongue-tied. And yes, you're right; he does have a photo of them together.

When Diana made number one in the charts there was a double-page spread in the paper about her, so I cut it out and sent it to Charlie. Doing little things like that is my way of keeping in touch, and letting the boys know I'm thinking about them. All grandparents have to work at it in order to nurture relationships.

Of course my grandsons aren't perfect — well, all right, they are perfect in my eyes; I might as well admit it. But even these perfect beings have their occasional moody spells. It's a common trait; watch out for that tricky early teenage period around 13 or 14 when they can sometimes be so monosyllabic in their replies — 'yup', 'nope', 'maybe', 'dunno'. 'How's school?' 'Fine.'

So much so that sometimes I hear myself saying, 'Are you purposely not talking to me, or are you just in a bit of a mood?' It can be hard work getting a response, and I'll find myself thinking, 'Am I being a total pain here, or is it them? Are you just tired, are you going through a hard time, or will I just stop talking here?'

What I've learned is that it pays to be patient, very patient, to have a thick skin and not to take offence or take it personally.

I've also learned that it really is a good idea to try to have some time with each of them on their own. That way you get more of a conversation, you get to find out what's going on for that particular child and to see a little deeper into their world. If I could go back and start again, one thing I would do is spend a little more time with each of my children individually. As a generality we always do things as a family, which is right and proper. But I also believe that children appreciate that one-to-one time, as I did on those Saturday mornings with my dad. It was having Dad to myself, not the ice-cream, that I loved most.

I always hoped I would be able to stay close to

the boys as they grew older. There was a tiny nagging concern at the back of my mind that they might be so busy with their lives that there wouldn't be room for me. But my worries have proved unfounded. Though the boys undoubtedly have hectic lives, and pack in a great deal, they always make time for us to meet and stay in touch. And I'm sure this is because we've been close from the beginning. But as they get older and busier I really do have to grow with them and make an effort to fit in with their lives.

I was interested to read a piece of research which found that, far from playing a lesser role in teenagers' lives, grandparents often play a particularly active role. Sometimes when things are a bit fraught between teenagers and their parents, they find it easier to talk to their grandparents, who are a good sounding-board, and not quite so close to the problem. They're more likely to understand both sides of a situation.

Parents often welcome the fact that their teenage children can and will talk to grandparents. Most parents obviously really love their children and only want the best for them, so if talking to a grandparent helps, rather than becoming resentful, parents are more likely to be relieved and pleased. If teenagers feel they can trust a grandparent and talk to them, it gives them a valuable independent outlet.

Grandparents can also help parents to see if they are being a bit draconian or are too rule-bound. One mum I know was laying down the law for her teenage son, who was becoming increasingly rebellious, the more rules he was given. When both the mum and the son turned to the grandfather for advice, he suggested that they agree just two rules to begin with — be home on time, and let your mother know where you are. The son agreed, and from this much simpler beginning the mother and son began to rebuild trust. The grandfather was able to step outside the immediate situation, and help find a solution for both of them. Sometimes experience can be truly valuable.

Let's be realistic: teenagers have a lot to cope with. They are concerned about everything: school, getting into university, what career to choose, relationships, sex and how attractive they are. They are curious about alcohol and drugs and through the internet they have access to potentially damaging websites and information. So a grandparent who can be a non-judgemental listening ear, offer hopefully wise advice and reassurance and remain calm and unflappable, can be a huge asset.

Grandparents must, of course, work together with parents, and not undermine or attempt to supplant them in anyway. So if grandchildren confide something that you think their parents really ought to know, encourage them to tell their parents, perhaps with you there to offer support.

Grandchildren will trust us, and want to be with us, if we accept them for who they are. We have to earn their trust. I always think that loving grandchildren is easy, because it tends to come naturally, in a huge wave, or sometimes creeping up on you by stealth. This new little being becomes, very quickly, the centre of your world. There's a lovely quote by an unknown author that says, 'If your baby is beautiful and perfect, never cries or fusses, sleeps on schedule and burps on demand, an angel all the time, you're the grandma.' Absolutely; that's because grandparents are allowed to dote — and we do, right through from the cradle to adulthood and beyond.

Another quote, also from an unknown author, says, 'Grandmas don't just say 'that's nice' — they reel back and roll their eyes and throw up their hands and smile. You get your money's worth out of grandmas,' which always reminds me of Beattie, the grandmother Maureen Lipman used to play in the BT ads — insistent that her grandson was a success, despite failing all his exams apart from pottery and sociology. How can I ever forget, 'You got an *ology*?'

When I was a young mother I used to think that if you got your children to the age of 18 reasonably unscathed, with good morals and a solid grounding, you'd done your job. How naive is that? It's only when your children are grown up that you discover the job of being a parent never ever ends, though it may change its shape. And you certainly never stop worrying about your children. Then, when you become a grandparent, you worry all over again, about your grandchildren. And you go on loving them and doing your best and hoping, as you did with your children, that you will always be able to be there for them.

One of the lovely things about being a

grandparent is that we are allowed to see only the best in our grandchildren. And that's valuable, because children need to have someone who, within reason, doesn't criticise, reprimand or chastise. Parents, even the most loving parents, have to do those things at times. But grandparents are — mostly — mostly — exempt. Author Phyllis Theroux said, 'We should all have one person who knows how to bless us despite the evidence; Grandmother was that person to me.'

That's the kind of grandmother I have always aspired to be. But then it's not just my story, it's that of millions of grandparents' all over the world, to be loving, accepting, encouraging, applauding from the sidelines, ridiculously proud, and always, always there for them.

Afterword

Soon after Caron gave birth to her first child — and my first grandchild — Charlie, she discovered these words from *The Prophet* by Khalil Gibran. This passage became one of her favourite pieces of writing and she had it pinned up over her desk wherever she lived. I love it too, not only because it reminds me so much of her but also because it is so wise.

Glorious Grandparenting is about children and grandchildren, and Khalil Gibran's timeless words remind us that our children and indeed their children are a gift from life. Our love for them guides and inspires us as much as we seek to be a guide and inspiration to them.

Your children are not your children.
They are the sons and daughters of Life's
 longing for itself.
They come through you but not from you,
And though they are with you yet they belong
 not to you.
You may give them your love but not your
 thoughts,
For they have their own thoughts.
You may house their bodies but not their
 souls,
For their souls dwell in the house of tomor-
 row,
which you cannot visit, not even in your dreams.

You may strive to be like them,
but seek not to make them like you.
For life goes not backward nor tarries with
    yesterday.
You are the bows from which your children
as living arrows are sent forth.
The archer sees the mark upon the path of
    the infinite,
and He bends you with His might
that His arrows may go swift and far.
Let your bending in the archer's hand be for
    gladness;
For even as He loves the arrow that flies,
so He loves also the bow that is stable.

Khalil Gibran

Acknowledgements

As with any publication, this book would never have come together without the help and support of so many people in all areas of life:

In this instance my first 'huge thankyou' goes to our grandchildren, who have brought such richness of fulfilment and fun to our lives, and without whom I would never have had the scope to write this book;

To our children who have given us the ultimate gift of grandchildren and the experience of extending the generations and family circle;

To Caro Handley whose research and dedication to the book has been totally invaluable; I could never have completed *Glorious Grandparenting* without her;

To the children of Curbar Primary School in Hope Valley, Derbyshire, for creating such delightful drawings and sayings about their grandparents;

To grandparents all over the country who have offered so much insight with their own stories, even though many sadly don't see their grandchildren;

I am totally indebted to everyone at Vermilion, especially Fiona MacIntyre, Managing Director, who had the inspiration for this book and the faith that we could address grandparents everywhere; to Susanna Abbott, Editorial Director, for her guiding judgement and real panache for deadlines; to Caroline Newbury, Deputy

Publicity Director, and to Louise McKee, Marketing Director;

To my literary agent, Eugenie Furniss, the demon negotiator as I call her; and to my manager, Laurie Mansfield, who is still the 'wise Buddha' and always there with his instructive advice and guidance;

And, finally, to all my family, friends and supporters of Caron's foundation, The Caron Keating Foundation, PO Box 122, Sevenoaks, Kent, PN13 1UB, www.caronkeating.org. My love and enormous thanks to you all.

Useful Contacts

Grandparents' Association
A membership organisation for grandparents. They run a helpline on 0845 434 9585. They also run local grandparents' support groups.
www.grandparents-association.org.uk

Grandparents Plus
A national charity which champions the role of grandparents and the wider family in children's lives. They run a national network for grandparents who are raising their grandchildren. Phone 020 8981 8001
www.grandparentsplus.org.uk

Grannynet
A grandparents' support and social networking website with tips on childcare and other issues.
www.grannynet.co.uk

BeGrand.net
An information and advice website for grandparents. You can join discussion groups, find useful information or contact an expert advisor.
www.beGrand.net

One Plus One
Provides a DIY online relationship support service offering personalised information and

advice which may be especially relevant for new parents and grandparents at www.thecoupleconnection.net

It also provides advice and support on co-parenting for separated parents at www.theparentconnection.org.uk

Parentline Plus
A national charity dedicated to helping anyone caring for children, whether you are a parent, grandparent or part of the wider family. Advice on any aspect of family life. Helpline on free-phone 0808 800 2222
www.parentlineplus.org.uk

Contact a Family
Advice, information and support for the parents of disabled children. They also produce a grandparents' guide for grandparents of disabled children. Helpline on 0808 808 3555
www.cafamily.org.uk

Family Action
Provides support services for families and works with the wider family as well as parents and children. Contact on 0207 241 7459, Tues, Wed and Thurs, 2–4pm.
www.familyaction.org.uk

Families Need Fathers
Runs a helpline for those who may be losing touch with their children or grandchildren and provides useful factsheets and information.

Contact 0300 0300 363
www.fnf.org.uk

Family Rights Group
A charity covering England and Wales which advises parents, grandparents and other family members whose children are involved with or require social care services. Confidential advice service on freephone 0808 801 0366.
www.frg.org.uk

Resolution
An organisation of family lawyers who support good practice in family disputes. They offer legal advice and support on their website and can find you a Resolution lawyer in your area. 01689 820272
www.resolution.org.uk

Young Minds
Runs a free helpline for anyone worried about the emotional problems or behaviour of a child or young person on 0808 802 5544
www.youngminds.org.uk

Mentor UK
Focuses on preventing drug misuse as part of a wider project to improve the prospects, health and wellbeing of children. Mentor UK's grandparents project seeks to advise grandparents on the harm that substance abuse can cause and how to make sure their grandchildren avoid it.
www.mentorfoundation.org

Marilyn Stowe
You can read the online blog of family lawyer Marilyn Stowe, who kindly helped with the legal information for Chapter 9, at www.marilynstowe.co.uk

We do hope that you have enjoyed reading this large print book.

Did you know that all of our titles are available for purchase?

We publish a wide range of high quality large print books including:
Romances, Mysteries, Classics
General Fiction
Non Fiction and Westerns

Special interest titles available in large print are:
The Little Oxford Dictionary
Music Book
Song Book
Hymn Book
Service Book

Also available from us courtesy of Oxford University Press:
Young Readers' Dictionary
(large print edition)
Young Readers' Thesaurus
(large print edition)

For further information or a free brochure, please contact us at:
Ulverscroft Large Print Books Ltd.,
The Green, Bradgate Road, Anstey,
Leicester, LE7 7FU, England.
Tel: (00 44) **0116 236 4325**
Fax: (00 44) **0116 234 0205**